WASTED?

PAUL SMITH

Know The Score Books Limited

www.knowthescorebooks.com

MOST SPORTS BOOKS tell tales of heroism and success. Guts and glory. Winning goals and golden rewards. Memories of a happy childhood with a cash-strapped but loving mum and dad doing their best for their talented kid despite all the odds. They'll include a couple of anecdotes from the Howard Keel Golf Classic and the author will pick their favourite team in the last chapter. It's biography by numbers. And it's bollocks.

If you're looking for that sort of book you should put this one down now. No doubt there'll be an Andrew Flintoff book within reach. Apparently a recent survey found that you are never more than ten feet from someone writing a 'Freddie' biography.

If you're interested in scratching beneath the surface of a life in sport, however, read on. If you want to learn about what happens when the cheering subsides, when the champagne has turned flat; when the prize money has been spent and when the sportsman has to leave the protective cocoon of the dressing room, then read on.

I can't promise a happy ending; this book is a cocktail of mixed and varied experiences - from drugs to divorce, the cult of celebrity to hedonism, adulation to fatherhood, desperation to glory.

Paul Smith
March 2007

WASTED?

PAUL SMITH

www.knowthescorebooks.com

**First published in the United Kingdom
by Know The Score Books Limited, 2007**

Know The Score Books Publications

CULT HEROES	Author	ISBN
CHELSEA	Leo Moynihan	1905449003
MANCHESTER CITY	David Clayton	9781905449057
NEWCASTLE	Dylan Younger	1905449038
SOUTHAMPTON	Jeremy Wilson	1905449011
WEST BROM	Simon Wright	190544902X

MATCH OF MY LIFE	Editor	ISBN
ENGLAND WORLD CUP	Massarella & Moynihan	1905449526
EUROPEAN CUP FINALS	Ben Lyttleton	1905449577
FA CUP FINALS 1953-69	David Saffer	9781905449538
FULHAM	Michael Heatley	1905449518
LEEDS	David Saffer	1905449542
LIVERPOOL	Leo Moynihan	190544950X
SHEFFIELD UNITED	Nick Johnson	1905449623
STOKE CITY	Simon Lowe	9781905449552
SUNDERLAND	Rob Mason	1905449607
SPURS	Allen & Massarella	9781905449583
WOLVES	Simon Lowe	1905449569

GENERAL FOOTBALL	Author	ISBN
BURKSEY	Peter Morfoot	1905449496
The Autobiography of a Football God		
HOLD THE BACK PAGE	Harry Harris	1905449917
WORLD CUP DIARY	Harry Harris	1905449909

AUTOBIOGRAPHY	Author	ISBN
TACKLES LIKE A FERRET	Paul Parker	190544947X
(England Cover)		
TACKLES LIKE A FERRET	Paul Parker	1905449461
(Manchester United Cover)		

CRICKET	Author	ISBN
GROVEL!	David Tossell	9781905449439
The Story & Legacy of the Summer of 1976		
MOML: THE ASHES	Pilger & Wightman	1905449631
WASTED?	Paul Smith	9781905449453

Forthcoming Publications in 2007

CULT HEROES	Author	ISBN
CARLISLE UNITED	Paul Harrison	9781905449095
CELTIC	David Potter	9781905449088
NOTTINGHAM FOREST	David McVay	9781905449064
RANGERS	Paul Smith	9781905449071

MATCH OF MY LIFE	Editor	ISBN
ASTON VILLA	Neil Moxley	9781905449651
BOLTON WANDERERS	David Saffer	9781905449644
DERBY COUNTY	Johnson & Matthews	9781905449682
MANCHESTER UNITED	Brian Hughes	9781905449590

GENERAL FOOTBALL	Author	ISBN
2007 VODAFONE CHAMPIONS LEAGUE YEARBOOK		
	Harry Harris	9781905449934
OUTCASTS	Steve Menary	9781905449316
The Lands That FIFA Forgot		
PARISH TO PLANET	Dr Eric Midwinter	9781905449309
How Football Came To Rule The World		
MY PREMIERSHIP DIARY	Marcus Hahnemann	9781905449330
Reading's Season in the Premiership		

CRICKET	Author	ISBN
MY TURN TO SPIN	Shaun Udal	9781905449422
LEAGUE CRICKET YEARBOOK		
Midlands edition	Andy Searle	9781905449729
North East edition	Danny Pugsley	9781905449712
North West edition	Andy Searle	9781905449705

Know The Score Books Limited
118 Alcester Road
Studley, Warwickshire, B80 7NT
Tel: 01527 454482 Fax: 01527 452183
info@knowthescorebooks.com
www.knowthescorebooks.com

A CIP catalogue record is available for this book from the British Library

ISBN: 978-1-905449-45-3

Jacket Design by Lisa David

Printed and bound in Great Britain by Cromwell Press, Trowbridge, Wiltshire

Mixed Sources
Product group from well-managed forests and other controlled sources
www.fsc.org Cert no. TT-TOC-2082
© 1996 Forest Stewardship Council
FSC

Contents

Photographs are reproduced with the kind permission of the Birmingham Post & Mail, Paul Davies, Kate Kelly, Graham and Diana Morris and Roger Wootton.

To Oliver, Mikey, Levi & Kizzi

Foreword

By Simon Donald

ONE DAY, at the age of 15, I stood in the stuffy, dark office of our school's deputy head, the diminutive and fearsome Miss Raby. She was sternly telling me how I was letting a lot of people down with my behaviour. Not least of all, my mother, who had been one of her best pupils in earlier years. She suggested that I took a few moments in silence to reflect on what I may become if my attitude towards school didn't change. It was a depressing and sobering experience.

As she faced me and stared straight at me, her eyes burned into my conscience. The silence was overbearing.

Until, that is, from immediately behind me, I heard the sound of the letterbox gently opening, followed by a voice bellowing, in the loudest and deepest Johnny Cash voice, "Big Don... Big Bad Don!"

The sound that followed I will never forget. It seemed to come straight from a cartoon, the likes of Scooby Doo or Deputy Dawg. It was the culprit desperately running on the spot, failing to achieve traction on the polished floor with metal 'segs' or 'Blakeys' in his shoes.

This all happened whilst Miss Raby was staring into my eyes. I failed to suppress my amusement, spluttering out a pathetic nasal exclamation. She strode purposefully past me towards the door, hoping to catch the offender before he got away. By the time she flung the door open the lanky perpetrator was 'surfing' on his segs around the corner of the corridor, windmilling his arms wildly in a vain attempt to keep his balance.

"Who was that?!" Miss Raby barked at me. "I've no idea, Miss," I replied, quaking inside with joy. I knew there and then it would make me laugh for a long time, and nearly 30 years on it can still put me in kinks. I knew very well it was Paul Smith.

'Smithy' and me always had a bond in humour. He loved to walk into a shop and ask how much an item cost. When told a Mars Bar cost 15p he would say, "So is that 15p each or three for 45p?" This made me laugh so much that we used it on the cover of Viz in 1985: "35p or 3 for £1.05".

Howling with uncontrollable laughter as we always did on our journey home from school one day, Smithy looked at me laughing in profile and suddenly exclaimed, "You've got a face like a shark!" as he fell off the kerb into the street, crying with mirth. He decided that from this point on he would call me Shark Face.

Despite our closeness we failed to keep in touch after we left school on the same day in June 1980 at the age of 16. Three years later Paul arrived unannounced at my first flat away from home. I was living with two other school friends and we were all unemployed. 'Smithy' snaked in dressed in burgundy leather trousers, having pulled up in a brand new car emblazoned with Warwickshire CCC graphics. He told us stories of glamour, success, fame, then he took us on a wild night out, before disappearing into the night, never to be seen again for 20 years.

In 2003 I got a message from another old friend called Angie who I also hadn't seen for years. At school she sat right next to 'Smithy' and me. She told me she'd bumped into him and they were now in regular contact. The next thing I knew I was asked by her to take part in a charity cricket match for Led Zeppelin guitarist Jimmy Page in Cambridgeshire. Whom had she booked as team captain? Only the man himself, my mate 'Smig'.

On meeting Paul after 20 years of separation it quite literally felt as if he'd just popped to the shops for a pint of milk. Absolutely nothing had changed. He only had to open his mouth and it would make me laugh.

But of course he hadn't popped out for a pint of milk, he'd spent 20 of the most colourful years having a brilliant sporting career and... well, what else besides?

I suppose it's time for you to find exactly what else he got up to besides, by simply reading this book. I don't know what he's written, but knowing Paul Smith as I do, the words that spring to mind are extreme, outrageous, shocking and not least of all, commendable.

It turns out the reason I let Miss Raby and everyone else down in my education was because I have a reading disability. I can comprehend written English very well, and write it, too, but reading is a horrible chore. So I'll not be reading this book myself. I'll wait for the audio book version to come out. Maybe it'll cost as little as £6.99, or 3 for £20.97.

Simon Donald
Co-Founder, Viz Magazine

Simon is currently working as a writer,
stand-up comedian, TV presenter and
full time media whore.

www.simondonald.com

Compton

"If you want to make God laugh,
tell him your plans."

I'D HEARD THE expression before, but never really thought about it too much. Now I truly understood.

I wasn't quite sure how it had come to this. I should probably have been playing professional sport back in England. I knew I could still have performed at that top level, and the team I had helped achieve unprecedented success was in the process of unravelling back home.

But I'd blown that and there was no way back, even if I'd wanted to find one. It was gone forever and I didn't miss it. Apart from financially.

So there I was in a park in Compton, Los Angeles, the part of L.A. renowned across the world for racial riots and regular gun crime. Tennis stars Serena and Venus Williams lost a sister in these parts; gunned down outside her own front door. Shit happens here - period.

For company I had an assortment of local kids. Mainly black, Latino or Hispanic, none of them with any previous cricketing knowledge. My role was to introduce them to a sport that had given me so many thrills and experiences globally. I'd come here to teach them the fundamentals of a game and, importantly its spirit and ethos; to provide some relief to their chaotic lives.

The place was hardly perfect. Gang warfare had driven a wedge through the core of the community. Casualties were plentiful. Within days I would be at the funeral of one of these kids; slain in a drive-by shooting. Within weeks I'd witnessed three kids buried.

Yet, for the first time in many, many years, I had a sense that this was where I belonged. Here was a place where I could make a difference. I had a fresh chance, without the considerable baggage I carried with me back home in England. I could start again; far from the prying eyes and the echoes of my mistakes. I knew immediately Los Angeles was where I'd end up living and working. A new life.

My experiences - good and bad - were all positive here. I could use them to connect with kids who would have been left cold by more formal techniques. They accepted me as one of them, someone who understood the way they lived their lives, the daily problems they faced of drugs and guns. I had a good feeling about this.

Back home I had been an outsider. I'd struggled to resist the lure of drugs. It had cost me my career. It had also cost me my family. I knew despair. I understood.

Working with these kids suddenly helped everything make sense. My ability to communicate with these young people on the fringes of society and at the crossroads of their lives helped them and me get back onto our feet. It was pretty ironic considering the relationship I was allowed with my own kids.

Yet, if life has taught me one thing, it is the truth of Thomas Hardy's words at the end of The Mayor of Casterbridge: "Joy is a brief interlude in a general drama of pain". This is the story of my journey to Compton.

The Drugs Don't Work

"If sporting authorities think they're controlling drug use with spot tests, they are living in wonderland."
Paul Smith, 1997

I STARTED TAKING DRUGS in early 1995. By that I mean I started taking them regularly in '95. I'd first taken cocaine at the start of 1984, but at that time I was busy. Drugs didn't interest me; even during the 20 weeks I'd just spent living in South America, a place where Pablo Escobar ran his cocaine distribution empire as publicly as Bill Gates runs Microsoft. My career and life were progressing pretty well and drugs just weren't on my agenda.

By 1995 things had changed. I was part of the most successful team in Britain and it was my benefit season. As a consequence I was obliged to attend a huge number of dinners and parties; far more than any of my team-mates.

Drugs were everywhere. Everywhere. Wherever I looked. Taking them seemed to go with the territory. Sometimes cocaine, but mainly ecstasy; MDMA (liquid ecstasy) to be specific. People think it's a dance drug. I don't dance, but I still saw plenty of it. I was never a huge fan of cocaine. As Robin Williams once said, "taking coke is just God's way of telling you you have too much money."

Whereas my home life was falling apart, I could be totally uninhibited when I was out. It was an escape from my real life. When I was socialising, everything altered for the better and the drugs fuelled that.

Dermot Reeve described me as 'cricket's first bimbo' and part of me is thankful for that experience. I learnt a lot about the opposite sex during the period and I'd be lying if I said some of it wasn't great. I believe you end up spending time with the women who want to be with you.

Life was exhausting. There was no `off time`. Not only were we giving our all physically on the field, playing more high pressure games than ever before, but the off-field demands were also draining. I was at a different event nearly every night, sometimes two. Australians refer to such events as 'crab pots' and I know exactly what they mean. Basically, it's easy to wander in but damn hard to leave. Often I'd return to the family home to find all the lights off and everyone in bed.

I really don't think drug problems would ever have occurred had it not been for Warwickshire winning a treble and my benefit season occurring in successive years. I don't think I was necessarily addicted to drugs. More addicted to the environments where they were taken. I was entering a time in life which continually led to a 'door of illusion'. This appeared to be a worry-free lifestyle: it was all very attractive, more 'free' women than I'd ever seen, an endless party and a chance to get away from things. The alternatives weren't appealing.

I desperately wanted to go home and see my two sons, but the relationship with my wife, Caroline, had pretty much broken down. That wasn't her fault; more a reflection that we'd married too young and grown apart. My continued absence didn't help. She was pretty much blameless for our marriage breakdown and we were divorced at the end of 1995. At that stage I would have done anything to put a smile on my face. And that's where drugs really came in. They helped blunt reality.

It's probably fair to say that I had started to hang out with the 'wrong' people. Not wrong as in flawed or neces-sarily bad, but just inappropriate for someone who earned his living as a sportsman. Michael Hutchence, the lead singer of Australian rock band INXS, was one such pal. We spent a few hedonistic days in each other's company. The charismatic singer was quite an avid cricket follower and I had actually met him for the first time as a youngster out in Australia. We were at the same dinner party in a house in Tourak, a trendy suburb of Melbourne, that started on a Sunday lunchtime and went on for the next 24 hours. The thing I remember most about that was that it was the first time I had ever been in the presence of people openly taking heroin. I reminded him about it when we met again a few years later.

Michael was wild. He appeared to have no boundaries and had an insatiable appetite for life. He took full advantage of the trappings of his success and made no attempt to resist the temptations in his path.

I very much enjoyed a couple of days we spent together in London at that time, but I'd be lying if I said I could remember too many of the details. Both of us were a little the worse for wear by the end of it. He had just finished his relationship with Helena Christensen and was young, free and single. Being handsome and rich has never been exploited so perfectly; we had a fine time.

At that time he exuded happiness and enthusiasm, but the lifestyle was to take its toll. By the end he was a shadow of the man he had been. His behaviour and moods became ever more inconsistent and the spirit inside him seemed to ebb away.

Drugs were certainly a contributor to his death, but in my opinion it was a bit more basic than that. He just loved experimenting. He wanted to experience everything, be it sexual, drugs or travel. Eventually, like many who live on the edge, he just went a step too far.

I hadn't really ever been worried about random drugs tests in my sport. Besides, for the bulk of my career I had no need to worry. By the mid-90s however, I just couldn't have cared what happened. My guard was down and I was susceptible to anything. I was also seeing my children less frequently, which gradually eroded all the responsibility and reasons for staying straight.

I remember one occasion in July 1996 when a drugs tester came to a game we were playing in Coventry. I was praying my name wasn't called. But looking back, maybe it would have been better if I'd been caught then. Certainly it would have been better for my health. I knew I was in trouble and a ban may have given me the kick up the arse I needed. I knew by then I had lost the plot and all I saw in front of me was a long descent. And the more I thought about it the more I wanted to escape those thoughts through taking drugs. I was weak.

In retrospect some good came from those experiences. I see lots of people - usually kids - going through the same things now. By recognising the signs and intervening at an early stage I've been able to advise and help some of them to avoid the hell that I saw. That was to become my aim in life a few years down the line. I'd like to think that by initiating professional lifestyle courses and tutorials, I've played a part in ensuring that some young people don't become victims and experience some of the problems I've been through. It also instilled a belief that sports clubs should evaluate the character of performers as much as their talent. If you want to ensure long-term results, you'll need sound individuals more than anything.

I wish someone had identified my problems in my early thirties. If I could have had the 1996 season off to get myself straight I think I could have contributed for another four years. As it was, I was seen as washed-up at just 32. Many players still have their best years ahead of them at that age; Graham Gooch, Alec Stewart, Peter Shilton.

I didn't feel I could even ask for help. The decision-makers at Warwickshire - in fact throughout the entire game of cricket - were straight from the Victorian era. Had I approached them and told them the full details, I would simply have precipitated my ostracism from the game. I was on my own.

It's not as if people hadn't clocked what was going on. I heard rumours. Several team mates - the likes of Tim Munton - later said that they were worried they would wake up one morning, turn on the news and find out I'd died in the night. In retrospect I think I'm lucky it didn't happen. Another team-mate stayed with me all night on one occasion in Birmingham, concerned about the amount of Ecstasy inside me, and my racing, irregular heartbeat.

The club must have known what was going on. I recall the Warwickshire coach, Phil Neale, now the operations manager with the England team, coming to talk to me. "I'm worried about you, Smithy," he said. "Are you alright?" "No problem," I replied "I'm great." But he knew, and he like a few others became increasingly reluctant to pick me for the side. Can't really say I can blame him, though even right at the end I knew I was still good enough. Even on my last pre-season tour, to South Africa in 1996, I took five wickets in a floodlit game against the only first-class opposition we faced. It was confirmed to me when I took 11 wickets for 64 runs in a 2nd XI match at Durham. I then travelled in excess of 1,200 miles in seven days with the first team, only to watch inferior performers selected in my place.

I never took a drug to improve performance; they were taken because I was desperate. Blank and vacant. Playing in a hugely successful team had done nothing in terms of self-esteem.

When I stopped taking drugs it didn't make me happy either. They don't do that. They enhance or destroy; they're never the full answer. Their effect on you is nearly always determined by other areas of your life.

A few people have asked me if I took cocaine during a tea interval in an Edgbaston NatWest semi-final versus Kent in our treble season of 1994. Leading up to a break I bowled erratically, conceding quite a few runs from my three or four overs at the City End. After the interval the captain, Dermot Reeve, immediately switched the end I was to bowl from, and my spell changed the game. It was as if I was a different man. Cocaine played no part in the action; you couldn't perform like that on it. My ability was to turn games when it was required; an ability to bowl repeated damn quick deliveries when it was needed.

The long spell of bowling proved to be one of the most draining of my career. It was powered by pure adrenaline and the desire to prove a point to those watching in the packed stadium. The following day, because of long-term knee problems, I could hardly walk. Later, even Dermot, my skipper, asked me if I'd had a line of cocaine when we'd come off the pitch at tea. It disappointed me that he asked. Still disappoints me. I never took a drug during or prior to any game in my career. Firstly, they wouldn't have worked and, secondly, I just would not have done so; I had too much respect for the game itself.

Marijuana later crept into my life as an alternative to alcohol, which was starting to lose its appeal. Drinking alcohol on top of taking Ecstasy allowed me to drink twice as much. Smoking marijuana was actually my attempt to rehabilitate myself; to calm myself down and combat the desire to go to a bar or late night restaurant. It makes you less energetic, even lazy, and I figured that might counter my natural inclinations. Brazilian footballing legend Romario said that "between the age of 18 and 30 I don't recall sleeping." I can identify with that.

I felt strong physically and remained hungry for excitement and adventure. Effectively the role of marijuana was to slow me down and make me stay in more. I knew that going out would lead to being in the presence of class A drugs. I knew I should try to do without them, but by then I was probably beyond help. Life was too fast and too furious. In truth, I'd been lost for the best part of a decade.

In this period I remember walking into a changing room the day prior to a Sunday game at Kent. It felt as if I'd walked into a conversation. It appeared to be about me. The next day in the fixture I was run out without fault when batting. I departed back up the motorway, knowing I needed the best advice. I also knew I wasn't going to receive it, despite the knowledge that an increasing number of players and coaches at Warwickshire were aware of my condition. When I got back to Birmingham a guy asked me if we'd won or lost. I couldn't remember.

I was aware of a lack of balance in my life. I knew that my lifestyle was affecting my preparation and my ability to perform as a player. I knew it was affecting all the other areas of my life, too. But, at that time, I wasn't strong enough to stop myself. Not without help, anyway.

The speed with which things changed was incredible. They say that drugs lose their appeal and became a habit and by the end of the '95 season they'd become a necessary part of any day. I was never more than 15 minutes away from cocaine. It wasn't that I wanted drugs particularly; I liked the lifestyle associated with them. Drugs entwined into life, the people with whom I associated, the places I frequented. It had stopped being fun. I felt my spirit dying.

My circle of friends altered, too. Whereas we used to meet for drinks as a team, the tight group dissipated. Our success split us. One guy would go home to his family as soon as a game was over, another to his flat on the other side of town. Others were dispatched to events in different corners of the city. I was spending fewer hours in a sound environment and, as a consequence, a few less savoury characters drifted into my life.

Maybe it seems as if I'm blaming other people for my mistakes. I don't think that's the case. I accept that I fucked up. But I do think that my experiences illustrate a lack of support mechanisms in the game. It excerbated problems that I accept I brought on myself.

People will always make mistakes. Sometimes when you're wrapped up in a team's performance, that is all you think about. Your only responsibility is to drive that team forward. On and on. You live only for that team. Many do this in business. My business was public, successful, and doors opened for me.

That's what had happened to me during the early 1990s. I didn't take the responsibility for myself that I should have. All my thoughts were occupied with work, only with me it was Warwickshire's success. Where I failed was in not recognising the importance of looking after my own life as well. I was defined as a person by my team's unique success. While I'm proud to have contributed to that, perhaps it masked problems in my own life.

At first I didn't think it affected my game particularly. Before a one-day match against Durham in early 1995 I had been enjoying an especially busy nightlife. Even by my standards, I was really going for it and hardly saw bed at all. Yet I still felt fit and strong and delivered my eight overs for just 13 runs; which still stands as a record in fixtures between the sides.

Adrenalin can hide pain and serious injury. In the short term, at least.

By the start of 1996 I knew I could take no more, however. Drug use had adversely affected my co-ordination and balance and the off-field problems were weighing heavy. I knew I had to get away from the environment. By July '96 I had told the club that I wanted to retire. Within months I was in Houston, Texas living a life of anonymity. No-one knew who I was when I went out there and the spell helped break the rut I was in, at least temporarily.

I'm not surprised newspapers found out about my problems. There were so many rumours about me. The details the press knew, however, could only have come from a very select group of people. The journalist who contacted me was pretty well informed about events that very few people could possibly have known about. They had stories linking me with taking drugs, promiscuity and nights on the town with all sorts of 'big name' cricketers and other celebrities. Some of the names were accurate, too accurate in fact. Some weren't. I've never sold any of my friends out. And I don't intend to start now.

If you read Jack Bannister's review of Warwickshire's 1997 season in *Wisden* it states that I made "lurid revelations" about my lifestyle. The version of events I agreed to have printed after a six-hour interview differed massively from the piece in the paper. Everything was sensationalised and it read as if I had just tried to earn 15 minutes of fame and a quick buck. Nothing could be further from the truth.

I certainly didn't sell my story. The way I saw it, a paper was going to print a story anyway. There was, for me, no way out. I was fucked. But some people implicated in the story - some of the biggest names in the game - could see their careers damaged if I didn't intervene.

I sought advice. I contacted a newspaper editor and a sports editor for their opinions. They conflicted, so I decided it was best to take the matter into my own hands.

I decided to try to kill the story by admitting my own guilt. I even admitted guilt for things I hadn't done. I took responsibility for absolutely everything. It was a form of damage limitation which effectively sentenced me to profess-ional death.

Even to this day, about a decade later, I am still judged by some on the content of that newspaper article. When Shoaib Akhtar was found to have failed a drugs test in 2006 many of the national newspapers printed stories about previous drugs problems in cricket. Most stated, incorrectly, that I had failed a drugs test. A couple of the senior writers later apologized to me for the mistake, but it does show how people jump to conclusions.

The ensuing ban I received from all forms of cricket was predictable. Some of those people I covered for have acknowledged it since; most haven't. Several are still involved in the game, some as coaches. They would have lost their careers had I spoken out against the injustice of it all.

I knew I had to stop taking drugs. I knew I was unwell and feared for my health, amongst other things. I suffered unexplained 'seizures' and was hospitalised. I'd suffered the symptoms of a heart attack. After waking up in my garden completely unaware of what had happened, I realised I'd blacked out on my feet. A doctor told me I had probably suffered an epileptic fit. Pains in my chest were growing more severe, and one morning I lost control of my car, swerving into a tree. I'd lost grip of the wheel as pains shot down my arms. It's fortunate the tree wasn't a person. All these things happened around the time of being banned.

The personal fall-out of my ban was catastrophic. The lost contracts struck like a knife, rendering it impossible to rebuild my life or to plan for a future, something I'd started doing 18 months earlier. Cricket was all I knew; all I'd done since I'd been a boy. Now I wasn't allowed to make a living from my profession, or even share the knowledge I had gained as a key member of the most successful team in the history of my sport.

Is this what Gerard Elias QC, the chairman of the England and Wales Cricket Board's (ECB) disciplinary committee, wanted? Did he realise that by cutting off my entire income, he was sentencing family life and my long-term prospects of rehabilitation to death? Or did he simply want to make an example of me? He might as well have put me in jail.

I had no chance of providing for a family. You do, I think, have to ask questions of a man who is prepared to throw people to the wolves quite so mercilessly. Nor have his decisions, as yet, been challenged, but I wonder at the lawfulness of robbing a human of his ability to earn a living.

I have considered my options over the issue. I have taken legal advice that suggests I would have a very good chance of success if I were to sue the ECB, but I'm still not sure I want to go down that path. It's not just about money. I would like to see Elias replaced and I'd like to set a precedent to ensure that nobody else goes through what I did. While I accept that the game has to make some statement about drug use, I cannot accept that the current policy is correct. Particularly when the drugs concerned are not performance enhancing. I had a problem, an addiction if you like, and the ECB responded with action that resulted in me losing my home, my life and my family. That's not a proportionate response. In fact, it's little less than cruel. When I needed help, they just added to my problems.

The reaction of some former team-mates hurt, too. Both my work and social life had gone in an instant and the loss of changing room culture took me by surprise. I'd thought I was part of something, but it turned out that it didn't actually exist. It proved to me that the support of most team-mates was limited to winning games of cricket. In retrospect it was probably naive of me to think anything else. Despite this, there is still more that unites the members of those Warwickshire sides than divides. There were just no support mechanisms. I suppose the episode showed me the way life really can be, also who and what friends are.

I was hardly the only cricketer to experience a problem with drugs. A well-known left-arm spin bowler is known to have climbed down a drainpipe at Essex's ground in Chelmsford in his (successful) attempt to escape drugs testers, while events close to home also raised questions. Another left-arm spinner, Richard Stemp, was let off after failing a drugs test that showed traces of Ecstasy in his system. Stemp claimed his drink was spiked and even produced the guy who admitted to have done the deed at his hearing!

Philip 'The Cat' Tufnell, now one of the BBC's top cricket personalities and renowned for becoming ITV's King of the Jungle in *I'm A Celebrity... Get Me Out Of Here!* also fell foul of the testers. It's little known that Tufnell smeared suncream into his eye to avoid being tested when the authorities turned up at Lord's unannounced one day. But it's true. Tufnell was fined £1,000 by his county, Middlesex, and reprimanded. But that was all. No lifetime ban for the Cat. He'd used up a couple of those lives of his.

In my own career I recall the drug testers arrived at Edgbaston and a team-mate being rushed from the ground and driven to our doctor. On another occasion our 12th man, Richard Davis, was sent to Holland and Barrett to buy a drink that, unknown to him, would help mask cannabis. The player then drove around with a flask of the drink in the boot of his car for the rest of his career. If the club wasn't implicit in a cover-up and aware of it, certain leading members of the side definitely were.

The player involved on both occasions was Keith Piper, who was twice banned for failing drugs tests in his playing career. Many, many people knew he was taking drugs during his career but chose to turn a blind eye while he remained a brilliant 'keeper. The hypocrisy of the situation was sickening. I was barred from making a living while he was able to continue as if nothing was wrong.

So I couldn't say I was shocked when stories of Dermot Reeve's drug use came to light in the summer of 2005. Reeve, my former captain at Warwickshire, admitted taking illegal substances. He also admitted to taking them during his years as a player, insisting, as I do, that he was far from alone in that. Stories of sex and drugs in unusual places made a double-page spread in a newspaper - The *Sunday Mirror* - that hardly finds space for cricket on other days.

There were many similarities between Dermot's situation and mine. Even the type of company was the same; a series of short skirts and coke companions. Like me, he was effectively the victim of a sting operation from a newspaper. Like me, he admitted taking drugs during his time as a player. And like me, he took the blame in order to cover for other people.

I met up with Dermot for a quiet drink the day the story broke. It was like looking in a mirror, albeit ten years previously. He wasn't in great shape. His cocaine habit had reached addiction stage and he had no idea where his life was heading. Later, when walking him back home, it became apparent he needed to get out of town. His fashionable canal-side apartment was situated in the middle of Birmingham's club and pub land. Temptation was everywhere. And he's hardly the resistant type. His lifestyle needed to change.

I'd changed my phone number a dozen times in as many months during my own period of transition. I needed to change my circle of 'friends'. I needed to break from the cycle that I was in; the lifestyle to which I had become accustomed. I needed to break from my past in order to create a future. I told Dermot all this. He'd told me how often he was going to the gym, trying to explain how he was managing the problem. "Makes no difference," I said. "A fit body is of no use if the head's not right."

During this period he was also helping and advising Piper, who had just been banned for the second time for drug taking. A case of the blind leading the blind. I saw Piper too. I spoke to him for the first time in three-and-a-half years. I'd made direct contact despite our history which, as you will learn, is 'complicated'.

Piper and I had been close friends for many years. We'd got to know each other well after he joined Warwickshire in the late 1980s and had experienced the good and the bad days together at Edgbaston. Unfortunately he ruined all that when he embarked on a clandestine relationship with my partner, the mother of my 5 year-old daughter, which caused the breakdown of that relationship.

The affair had been underway for the best part of four years before I found out. One night in 2001 I put my daughter in my car and drove to Piper's Edgbaston apartment only to find my partner's car parked by his. Suddenly it dawned on me what had been going on. I had been naive in the extreme, though in my defence I had been working long hours with the aim of providing one house where all three of my kids could come and spend as much time as they liked.

When the penny dropped I sent a text to both parties and left a message on Piper's answer machine telling him to ring immediately. It took him six weeks. I immediately drove back home in pouring rain, in total silence, whilst my daughter slept. Two hours later there was a knock on my front door and in burst my partner's mother. Within seconds my daughter was taken away from me, even though she was clearly upset and confused. I watched as she was driven away, out of my life. She was gone.

Because the breakdown of the relationship was messy, I was denied custody of my daughter. I was denied any access at all. Though I don't believe Piper deliberately wanted that to happen he went along with it as it was easier than arguing with his partner. He let me down. As someone who hadn't been brought up by his own parents, and had a real hang-up about that, Piper should have known the effect his actions would have on my daughter's life.

Though there have been times since when I've been allowed to have contact with my daughter, my former partner has put every obstacle in my path to stop it from happening. As I write this it is over two years since I have even seen my daughter. I don't know where she lives, where she goes to school or have any means of making contact. At times I've been told she no longer lives in Great Britain. That is not something that I find easy to live with.

The pain of discovering the infidelity still hurts. More importantly, it still affects everyday life. I guess my ex-wife, Caroline, from whom I had been divorced for over six years at this point, would say that I was simply experiencing what I deserved. And I guess she has a point. But it is

A BEAUTIFUL DAY FOR A WEDDING

Gladstone Small was my best man and went down a storm. His speech had everyone in stitches. The day after the wedding I walked out to bat with 'Here Comes The Bride' being sung, only to walk back just seconds later having been dismissed first ball.

Not an auspicious start... It was a hectic period. Adapting to married life at such a young age and then our first child arriving soon afterward was hard. I willed myself to stay a teenager. In retrospect I don't think we ever had much of a chance. Perhaps if we'd met a few years later it might have worked better. Or if we had known each other a little better. In certain ways I believe you never stop loving the women with whom you have children. It's umbilical. Caroline and I exchanged harsh words at times and I'm sure she's felt exasperated by

me, that's not my intent, but there should be more that unites us than divides. Sometimes good intentions aren't enough, though, and not everything that counts can or has been counted.

Looking at the picture, the expression 'smile like you mean it,' comes to mind. It doesn't look the most relaxed scene, does it? Caroline and I married the day after a quarter-final game that had threatened to spill over into a second day. It seemed to sum everything up; there wasn't time to think things through and my priorities were far from clear. From a selfish perspective it wasn't easy to concentrate on cricket with a young bride and young children needing attention. That's not a regret. My children are the best thing that's happened to me. The kids actually made life worthwhile. Watching kids grow is one of life's greatest gifts.

I'm not sure anyone involved in sport can give their best once they have a family. Parents have to make compromises and, all too often, both the career and a family can lose out. More recently I made contact with my former mother-in-law more than a decade after my divorce from her daughter. Afterwards I wished I had done it years before. We had differences in the past, but agreed on much more than we disagreed. Our intentions for the children are the same and we have the same beliefs about the importance of fatherhood.

somewhat ironic that my relationship with the mother of my daughter was monogamous. Or at least I thought it was!

There's even more irony when I recall the timing of my discovery. Piper's benefit season had just been launched two days before and, despite growing financial troubles, I had put a £20 note into his collection. I thought he was a close friend. Clearly I was wrong.

Anyway, soon after the news of Dermot's drugs problems hit the papers, he flew out to Australia to 'work' at his marriage. The best guys to go out for a drink with often make the worst husbands. Even if his wife wouldn't take him back, he was still able to work things out with his kids. I knew from experience that this would be a long and painful process and wished him well. But first he had to learn to control a drug problem.

The episode has damaged Reeve's ability to work in cricket. He had told me even before Channel 4 fired him that his commentary work had lost its appeal, but his enthusiasm for coaching remains undimmed. I don't think he ever wanted to stop coaching. He enjoys the 'hands on' nature of the job. But the lure of the media spotlight - and the money on offer - proved irresistible to a man who has always revelled in attention. Indeed, he accepted a job as Yorkshire coach at the end of 2004 before the club changed their minds. He still got paid.

It will be interesting to see how Elias reacts if and when Dermot tries to return to cricket. Elias, chairman of the ECB disciplinary committee, never had a chance to pass sentence on Reeve and if Elias is the man I think he is, that may irk him.

In 1997 I attended a disciplinary committee chaired by Elias to fight for my career. The sports agent, Jonathan Barnett, who represented me that day, pleaded for clemency. He said that I was a father of three young kids, one just born, and that to remove my earnings would have drastic effects on my entire family. He said that more than punishment, I needed help.

Maybe Elias listened. Maybe he had his mind made up even before he got up that morning. I was sentenced to a

22-month ban. I was numb. Later, when I asked for a recorded copy of the hearing I received a blank tape!

Half-an-hour after being banned I was offered 90 grand to talk to a tabloid journalist. Had I done so it would have split the fucking sport. Barnett, who brokered the deal with the paper, lost interest in me after that. I guess money was his main motivation. Fair enough.

I still loved the game - still do - and didn't want to see it further besmirched. Nor did I want to see friends and team-mates placed in the same position as me. There are people still involved in the game who don't appreciate the sacrifice made that day.

The financial consequences of the ruling were dire. Within weeks I'd lost two playing contracts, an equipment sponsorship deal and two roles promoting companies. I had no money coming in. It was a hero to zero situation.

A decade later, Dermot flew out of the UK without a ban. Maybe society has become more tolerant to drug use. Most people know that recreational drug-taking - among young people, at least - is as commonplace as a visit to the pub for an older generation.

The ECB have remained with their heads in the sand, however. Their 'zero tolerance' attitude has created a rod with which they have thrashed themselves regularly. The ICC - world cricket's governing body - hasn't even been testing for cannabis, nor have the West Indies or the Australian cricket boards. Why? Because it's irrelevant, or because they think it's best not to peer too deeply beneath the surface?

Yet the ECB remain steadfastly set on a hopeless crusade. Their policy, at present, is a bundle of contradictions wrapped up in a dilemma. There is no consistency in the bans they hand out. They insist that cricket will remain utterly drug free, even of border-line recreational drugs such as cannabis. They may as well try to hold back the night. Young cricketers will surely reflect the society from which they emerge.

It may surprise some, but I actually agree with the ECB's stance. It's just that they don't go about it the right way.

Their approach isn't realistic or, as a consequence, effective.

In recent years the Professional Cricketers' Association (PCA) and the ECB have got together and sent representatives around the clubs to warn players about the dangers of drug use. The problem is that the personnel have been ill-suited to the task. Tim Munton, for example, was one of those chosen for the task. Tim's a decent, well-meaning man. In many respects he is a perfect role-model and a guy who deserves a lot of respect. But you might as well send your grandmother out there for all his knowledge of the subject. I think it is a role I could fulfill; warning players of the pitfalls of drug use and suggesting support and intervention when necessary. It's fairly obvious when you've been there.

Young people take drugs, period. Those that play lots of sport probably have less time to do so; but there are no guarantees. I once played a social game of sport with a bunch of guys whose occupations varied drastically. Computer sales; radio; marketing: makes no difference. Most of them enjoyed smoking marijuana occasionally; it doesn't mean that those occupations are full of drug addicts. Avoidance is happiness and freedom, the very thing drug users think they gain when things kick in.

There are a lot of inquisitive people watching to see what happens if and when Reeve returns to professional sport. Elias is waiting for him and its doubtful Reeve could take up a job without answering some sort of disciplinary hearing. I believe that Dermot called Elias after the story broke to have an unofficial conversation about what to expect should he attempt to return to coaching. Wouldn't it be refreshing if the game recognised the context of Reeve's position? He is a man who has been ill and needs rehabilitation. He requires help, not punishment.

Yet there are people in the media - people who harbour resentments against Reeve for tiny sleights they feel he made maybe a decade or more before - who will kick up such a fuss that the ECB are obliged to act. Otherwise they will be open to charges of inconsistency. Better to be right once than consistent always, though.

It will take a leap of faith from a county to back Dermot, but his record is impressive. As captain of Warwickshire and coach of Somerset he achieved much. It would be a damn shame if his talents were lost to the game.

Of course, if Dermot were a bigger name, he'd probably be fine. It appears that the punishment depends on a player's importance within the game of cricket.

When Shane Warne failed a drugs test and was sent home on the eve of the 2003 World Cup, there was a fear that his career might be over. Yet although the Australian cricket board had a minimum two-year ban for such an offence, Warne was eventually banned for just 12 months.

Warne was found to have taken a diuretic - a mixture of hydrochlorothiazide and miloride - designed to promote weight loss. He claimed he'd taken a pill offered by his mother in an attempt to lose fluid as he tried to regain his fitness following a recently dislocated shoulder. A stupid mistake, basically.

But what was not widely understood is that the tablet Warne took can also be used as a masking agent. It can dilute traces of steroids in the urine and help guilty athletes get through drug tests undetected. Dick Pound, who headed WADA (World Anti-Doping Association) at the time, was furious at the lenient treatment shown to Warne and went so far as to call him "a cheater".

A similar situation occurred in late 2006 when Pakistan fast bowlers Shoaib Akhtar and Mohammed Asif were both found to have taken nandrolone. Although the pair were subsequently banned from cricket for two years and a year respectively - absurdly unfair as they had been found to have committed the same crime - they were both then cleared on appeal. Although neither of them disputed that traces of the steroid were found in their bodies, they claimed that it must have been present in supplements taken in good faith; a reasonable enough explanation, perhaps. Except that WADA rules insist that's irrelevant. Athletes are expected to take responsibility for what goes into their bodies. There can be no excuses.

Shoaib Akhtar was, initially, vilified. He has not always toed the line and there were some that seemed to take the opportunity to put the boot in. One of the original three-man panel who recommended the playing bans, Intikhab Alam, said this of Shoaib: "He drinks alcohol, has an active sex life and he's been part of an anti-doping awareness program." So what? Does that prove he was guilty? I can assure Intikhab that Shoaib is far from the first of his countrymen to enjoy the delights more normally associated with Western culture. It reminded me of my own experiences. I had long hair and everyone knew I liked a night out; sometimes people make judgments long before they meet you. Sometimes if you play around people misunderstand the playfulness for indiscipline.

There were several inconsistencies in the pair's tests. Forms were not filled in properly and there was confusion as to which urine sample was Shoaib's and which was Asif's. Nor have Pakistan actually signed up to the WADA code of practice.

At the time of writing, the pair are awaiting the outcome of another appeal launched by WADA. Some would say they are unfortunate victims of a sport still struggling to come to terms with a nebulous issue. Others would say they are simply cheats, trying to gain an unfair advantage over their opposition and living by different rules to the rest of the world's cricketers and athletes. All I would say is that I was banned from cricket after a newspaper article said I had taken recreational drugs. These guys have actually failed tests that suggest they had taken performance-enhancing drugs.

Immediately prior to the start of the 2007 Cricket World Cup, Shoaib and Asif both, astonishingly, broke down injured. Coincidence? Meanwhile Warne is lapping up the plaudits as his Test career ends in the glory of having become the first test cricketer to take 700 wickets.

Shane Warne and Shoaib Akhtar sell their sport like few others; right up with the likes of Sir Donald Bradman. The sport is certainly greater for their involvement. I've no reason to doubt their word. But where's the consistency?

Just a year after Warne's problem, Warwickshire all-rounder Graham Wagg suffered a longer ban when he was found to have taken cocaine, a recreational drug in no way, shape or form performance enhancing. Wagg was banned for 15 months. Elias was again chairman of the disciplinary committee. Warwickshire fired the 21 year-old Wagg from their staff and banned him from coming to the ground. He was unable even to take his coaching badges.

Wagg was not just banned from playing in the UK. When he tried to rebuild his career by playing club cricket in Holland, the Dutch cricket board banned him too, though he was, somewhat perversely, able to continue coaching children. Some say he received no help from Warwickshire, the PCA or the ECB for the first year of his ban, though the PCA later played a key role in helping him restart his career. This despite the fact that he had been involved with Warwickshire since he was a young boy and that he had been part of the previous England Academy tour, playing three youth Test matches against India. The game washed its collective hands of him. They couldn't have given a toss.

What did they expect Wagg to do? The truth is they didn't care. He screwed up, sure. But he isn't a guy blessed with many options. Brought up on a tough estate in Rugby, cricket was the one thing that kept him on the straight and narrow. For the sport to take away his best hope of salvation wasn't constructive. It was cruel. I would have thought it was also contrary to the 'spirit of cricket'. He has done well to earn another chance with Derbyshire, but it will take a very strong personal effort if he is to make it in the professional game.

Some on the Warwickshire committee declared that Wagg had disgraced the club and that he would return "over their dead body". Nobody took responsibility. Nobody reflected that Wagg was a product of the Warwickshire system and that there was a duty of care to a former employee; particularly one which they had supposedly developed in his formative years.

Interestingly enough, almost simultaneously, Chelsea's Adrian Mutu received only a six-month ban when he was found guilty of taking the same drug after the club carried out in-house testing. He was also paid during most of his ban. Remarkably, the London club was fined 40k by the Football Association for administrating this drug test. Chelsea claimed the FA was more interested in procedures than substance. Later down the line heavyweight World Boxing Champion Frank Bruno admitted to using cocaine and marijuana, while sprinter Mark Lewis Francis failed a drugs test for cannabis and received no ban at all.

A short while after Wagg was hauled in front of Elias's committee; in fact the very first game of the following cricket season, Warwickshire's experienced wicket-keeper Keith Piper failed the second drugs test of his career. He had been recalled to the first-class team after an 18-month break and perhaps hadn't taken the normal precautions. He received a relatively short ban; four months. That reflected the relative soft nature of the drug - cannabis - and his West Indian culture. Cannabis, it was argued, is a commonly taken drug in that community. Some would argue that ecstasy and cocaine were commonly taken drugs on the Rugby estate in which Wagg was raised, but the sport's not ready to accept such truths.

People who want help are scared that if they sought assistance it would be held against them and ruin their career. A few youngsters who'll rightly remain anonymous told me so. After all, who am I to risk their careers? But there's no doubt, it's a developing scandal which cricket is singularly failing to cope with.

Amongst all the myriad of comments made at the time this was one of the most telling. Ian Smith, the Professional Cricketers' Association's lawyer, who repre-sented Piper at the disciplinary hearing, talking to George Dobell of the *Birmingham Post*, said:

> *"Warwickshire knew at least eight years ago that Keith Piper had a drugs problem. They were like a parent who suspected that their daughter has just started sleeping around; they had fears but didn't want to find out the whole truth. They never confronted him because they were terrified about what they might discover."*

Spot on, although I think they'd known even longer than that. Several years earlier - in the 1990s - I'd actually written a letter to Warwickshire's then Chief Executive Dennis Amiss warning him about Piper's drug use. After Piper first failed a drugs test in 1997, I told him that they couldn't have tested all the players if that had been the only positive test. I spoke to Amiss again in 2001, both face to face and by telephone.

Many people at Warwickshire knew about Piper's habits. Not only had I warned them, senior players and members of the coaching staff had also warned the club's chief executive that Piper's 'lifestyle' was causing concerns.

Even when Wagg was banned from the ground they knew about Piper but preferred to remain quiet. After all, he was a very good wicket-keeper. Maybe the best; certainly with England potential. Later this inaction was to come back to haunt the club.

In 2005 it was finally publicly acknowledged that I'd covered for several players at the time of my ban, and that effectively it had merely served to cover for everything that had come to the surface since. It was an acknowledgment that came way too late to help me or those other players hooked on drugs, though.

I wish Keith Piper well. He has undergone extensive counseling and rehabilitation and faces a fight to get his life back on track. Despite the history between us I hope he comes through it. It will be desperately hard, not just in the short term but for the rest of his life.

I remember sitting in such counselling sessions. It's easy to say the right things in a quiet room in a clinic. At the time you mean them, too. It's just you, a pot plant and a councillor and you think it will be alright.

It's not real, though. The second you're outside then all the pressures come rushing back at you. Temptation is everywhere. It's hard to remain strong all the time. By all accounts Piper has started well. He has recently been appointed as Warwickshire second XI coach and appears to be the man that the director of cricket, Mark Greatbatch, turns to for advice. Piper's energy and optimism have made a positive impression at Edgbaston, though he has a long and tough road to travel on his journey.

For many years I got on with Piper very well. We were team-mates for a long time, of course, and shared a lot of happy experiences off the field. That's part of the reason I was so disappointed. In many ways I feel his treachery was more disloyal than that of my daughter's mother. He should have known better. There is still some fondness there when I think back to shared experiences, but it's very difficult to see him even now.

We'd shared a lot of laughter. I recall going to a night-club in Trinidad with him and the great Australian batsman, Mark Waugh. I had to say I was Mark's Australian team-mate, fast bowler Mike Whitney, while Piper said he was the scorer. All night the locals told me what a terrible tour I was having; what a rubbish bowler I was. "Hey Whitney; concentrate on your batting."

Three hours later we left only to see the real Mike Whitney arguing with the doorman. "Whitney is inside already," the doorman was saying. "Just go home." To rub salt into his wound, we then took the Aussie team limo back to the hotel. It was a fun night. But it was a long time ago. A lot has happened and it can't be undone.

Cricket's problems are minor compared to other sports. Masking agents are used frequently in certain sports. The image of cycling has suffered badly, as has American Football and Baseball. Olympic athletes such as Ben Johnson and Justin Gatlin, in tandem with coaches who are fully aware of the colossal financial rewards success brings, have tainted their sport.

Have you noticed how times in athletics have generally stopped improving over the last couple of years? That trend has coincided with the great advances made in the testing procedures by the anti-doping bodies. New technologies have made it harder for drug cheats to get away with it. Coincidence? I don't think so.

Remember, Florence Griffith Joyner retired four months after random testing was introduced! The winner of three gold medals at the Seoul Olympics, she forged a great career after sprinting out of the ghetto in which she was raised for finer pastures, but was her death at the age of 38 the price to pay? Do you think that there won't be further victims down the road?

Dick Pound recently said he believed that the market for sports supplements - many of which contain small quantities of 'banned' drugs - was bigger than the entire market for recreational drugs. He also said that "only the stupid" get caught and made special mention of cricket as a sport with a great deal to do before it could be said to be tackling the issue effectively. The problem is huge and growing. But just as is the case with alcoholism, sport needs to accept it has a problem before it can start to deal with it.

Things within cricket have improved somewhat. There are better support mechanisms for players now. Quite recently a county batsman - one who might well have had a future at the highest level - received sympathetic support from the PCA and his county after a failed suicide bid. But surely it would have been even better to intervene before he tried to kill himself?

Youngsters entering my sport should get as much life mentoring as coaching. A trained eye will see a weakness. Better to teach avoidance habits when the young player is all ears and bright-eyed. Counties should invest in mentoring and monitoring as much as coaching.

The governing body's attitude to recreational drugs strikes me as bizarre. If we accept that a drug is not performance-enhancing, then why are we banning players? It can only be for moral reasons. So are we going to start banning players convicted for speeding? For infidelity? A good case could be made to say that drink driving is a far more serious crime, yet I'm not aware of a player ever being suspended for such a misdemeanor despite the fact that several such unfortunate occurrences have undoubtedly taken place.

Recently entertainers such as George Michael and Graham Norton spoke openly about their drug use, but nobody has stopped them working. They are role models to many, yet the suggestion that they be banned from appearing on our televisions or radios is absurd. Different rules exist for sportsmen than the rest of society it would appear.

Divorce exacerbated my problems. A huge amount of money was wasted, mainly through an inability to sort things out face to face. My ex-wife was angry, I can understand that, and I had to leave the family home. The sight of two adults at the end of a relationship was not one I wanted my children to see. I knew divorce would be hard but I failed to forecast the magnitude of the varied reaction which came at me.

My children were all that kept me straight. In a world that was, for me, increasingly bleak, they were the only rays of sun. They were all that mattered; the only thing that made sense, but now they had been taken from me. The lack of contact with them was the hardest thing to take. No longer could I take them to the park, or walk them into school. My only contact with healthy society was closed to me. Of all the pain I've experienced, nothing else compares.

Generally in life, when I've had money, I've been able to see my children. Once the legal profession tucks in, however, it erodes your resources quite quickly. I was bombarded by demands. It may have appeared to the mothers of my children that I was simply reluctant to pay my share, but that's not fair. The truth is that I ran out of money. As a result there was a reluctance to let me see the kids. The experience of being denied taught me a lot.

It suited other people for me to be portrayed as a poor father. True, I've probably not been the father I should have been, but barriers were put up to stop me. Having spent the bulk of my post-playing career working with kids, it's ironic that I haven't seen as much of my own as I'd have liked. I just hope my children have always known and understood how much they're loved.

My appreciation for Fathers For Justice has become immense. Those that have seen how the divorce system works against men will know how inequitable it is. Only those who have experienced the injustices of the Child Support Agency or the frustration of having your children kept from you will truly know the pain I'm talking about. It's unbearable.

From a family home - albeit an imperfect one - I now lived in a soulless city apartment. I lived 'a footballer's life'. I had too much time on my hands.

My abiding memory of the whole period is the smell of alcohol in venues closed to the public. Dirty deeds in dirty places. It brought the worst out in me. There is, I suppose, something liberating about abandoning yourself to chance, but my only real motivation was escapism.

I didn't want to lose contact with my children. I never divorced them. I recall wasting time in front of a judge in Birmingham, being told to walk my children to and from school, to greet my ex-wife with glee and to watch as the door was shut on me. It was a time of play-acting, a time when there was an endless drain on bank accounts and nothing going back in. Within a matter of months I found out I was to be a father again. It was the first female birth in my family for 90 years; a beautiful daughter. My little girl that I was to lose within six years.

A few years later I spent much of the summer taking my little girl to stay regularly at a friend's castle, a privilege which came with at least knowing some people who stuck by me when all else was going wrong in life. The access to my daughter coincided with me being able to see my two boys and it was wonderful to spend time together. They were happy days, but all too brief. I cherish the memories, but they also bring pain. They remind me of time lost; time I'll never get back.

Wasted?

Cricket Without Boundaries

I'M HARDLY THE FIRST to lose my way. I won't be the last either. Increasingly I came to a realisation that society is full of people who feel they don't fit in. I wonder if everyone feels that at some point in their life. It was certainly the way I felt as my professional playing career came to an end. There didn't seem to be much out there for me. I knew I wanted to make some sort of difference and do good work, but couldn't really claim that I had control of my own life.

Then came the realisation: by helping others I could also help myself.

I came up with the concept of Cricket Without Boundaries when I was in the USA. Once every thing was lost and long gone in England I spent a lot of time in the States. It was about escapism, really. I wasn't seeing my kids and in America I could pretend everything was ok. There weren't the usual sights and sounds to remind me of what I had lost and I kept myself occupied so I didn't have to reflect too deeply.

Texas proved a place of great education. The Lone Star State is known for many reasons. Its people, especially Houstonians, are different to others you might meet any-where, even within the U.S.. Seen as the execution capital of the States, here you'll find yourself meeting incredible characters resembling Dog the Bounty Hunter, a well-known media personality over there, who will do anything for you - if the price is right.

In the U.S. I could live any life that I wanted. It was all very rock 'n' roll. Money and women; I got through them both as if there were no tomorrow. I can't honestly say I regret it. I was finding mself again. I mingled with various hi-rollers with apparently wildly successful careers behind them. They were the sorts of people who would casually ask if you're interested in investing 10 million dollars in their latest oil-drilling venture. I learnt quite a lot.

The name Cricket Without Boundaries was born at a baseball game; it just came to me. All around America I saw things and attitudes which later helped round its delivery. I also saw how if people did well, others were pleased for them. In reality it seemed an easier place to get on. A real living land of opportunity.

In Houston I saw how court order probation restrictions forced individuals to attend courses or activities. These courses all used some sort of different sport or skill to engender change and I listened to the details of how the courses were delivered and the methods of dealing with awkward customers. Later in California during one session involving cricket, a team leader, worried at handing a cricket bat to a convicted young felon, said, "Are you seriously expecting me to put a 3lb piece of wood in his hands?"

Having watched different types of delivery the rest was easy. Writing my proposal for Cricket Without Boundaries (CWB) came within a week. I made three phone calls and went to see some existing training sessions in a dog rough area of Houston. The level of their funding depended on the age, zip code and type of crime, also the character of the individual.

I also spent some time at the University of Austin. Their library people explained the basics of funding and the different foundations that could provide it. It wasn't all goggle work; I met a lot of people. Although the specific knowledge was applicable to Texas, the fundamentals applied virtually everywhere. I also knew by this stage that if I wanted to be part of something in America it would be in California where my contacts were better. The relationship I had been in had produced a little girl, but from early on it was apparent that the mother and I would part. I was on my own and realised that I had to plan without fear or compromise.

By this stage I'd already met Tim Watts, the chairman of Pertemps Group. This happened a few months after Gerard Elias had seen fit to prevent me from earning a living from the only way I had ever known how. Tim and I talked about my future employment possibilities and what I thought I could do well. He was willing to help me put an end to my recent past.

People think I went to see Tim Watts because he has a lot of money. I didn't. I went to see him because of the type of concept I had. If I'd wanted to start an ice cream or sweet shop I'd have visited contacts at Cadbury in Bournville for advice. Watts's potential funding streams covered most employment and training concepts, or kids' community activities. More importantly, he believed in the overall concept.

There were a couple of years between that initial conversation with Watts and the next time I visited him. In that period I worked in loads of schools and at a lot of community facilities and clubs. I watched, I listened and I learned. I learned which words consistently pressed the right buttons with the kids and which words pressed the right buttons in terms of gaining funding. I worked out a robust method of delivery. I applied Bob Woolmer's coaching methods and the communication skills picked up from explaining cricket to Americans. I utilised my own experiences of winning and losing; of being on top of the heap and bottom of a pile; of loss and exasperation.

The package had come together by the time I went back to Watts. The scheme works like this: people were referred to Pertemps Employment Alliance (now Pertemps People Development Group) via the employment agencies - or unemployment agencies as they should be called. We had three months to find them work, taking them off government assistance. Each client referred came with a budget of roughly £4,000 - for example - and each week that the client remained on our books ate into that money. Out of it came the purchase of suits, transport costs, clerical support for job interviews; whatever it took we tried to deliver. It worked. Pertemps received the remainder of the money left in the account after each client had re-entered the workplace.

There are a number of agencies that distribute money to bodies working with the socially excluded. Usually the funding is distributed regionally, particularly into communities which have problems. The PCA also agreed to help me and I persuaded Sport England in London to invest for a minimum of three years. These monies helped pay salaries, train and qualify new coaches, buy kit; training shoes, tracksuits and tops. It also paid the hire charges for sports halls and community centres.

The idea was to use cricket as a tool to motivate and retrain the long-term unemployed. The only criteria was that recruits had to have been unemployed for four-and-a-half years. When out of work for that long, it's easy to give up. There are only so many rejections one can take. Eventually you stop trying. Any confidence that was ever in existence drains away. People are left with an overpowering sense of worthlessness. The routine of unemployment has taken over.

These courses were a lifeline. I witnessed the most introverted people come out of their shells and learn to work with their new colleagues. It was an inspiring experience. It was also eye-opening. I saw how many people in society were affected by alcoholism, drug intake and addiction, also the side effects of physical abuse. I saw how many people had gained little from all their years of state education, and how the safety net of the state was wholly inadequate. It just deals in short-term solutions. If someone has an infection, doctors try and fight it; but they don't attempt to change the lifestyle of the patient in order to prevent further problems. If someone's unemployed then they are corn-fed a small sum of money to keep the wolf from the door; there's often no effort to solve the underlying problems. I wanted to see if it was possible to empower people to rebuild their lives.

There's often no point putting these people straight into a classroom. That's an environment which immediately alienates them. Many of them have probably never shone in a classroom, and to put them straight back in that setting reminds them of previous failures. There's initially not much point in getting them to talk to each other either. They usually have little self-confidence and their communication skills have suffered through long periods of inactivity. They are damaged.

Activity needed to be structured for them to avoid boredom and to boost their confidence. It needed to be enjoyable; fun yet constructive, disciplined yet relaxed. It had to make people inquisitive. But it wasn't essential for them to have any previous knowledge of cricket, indeed necessarily of any sport at all.

A typical day on a course would start with some sort of discussion. There would also be some sort of light paper work; those who couldn't read or write would receive help or encouragement. We would have a couple of five-minute breaks every hour or so, and lunch would be provided. The importance of providing free food shouldn't be underestimated; I'm sure that for some it was initially the primary motivation in attending. The afternoon sessions revolved around sport. We were trying to make them more attentive. The day would always conclude with a game lasting up to an hour. It always proved popular as people came out of their shells and helped form a bond within the group.

Over time the delegates would learn the basics of communication, learning to trust the call of a batting partner, for example. They would learn the importance of encouraging the fielders and the bowlers and learn how good it felt when someone said to them 'well done'. They might also find that it felt good to say it back occasionally, too. Each pair batted for a guaranteed period of time to ensure their full involvement. Over time they became more confident, backed their own judgment and began to focus rather than just exist. That confidence worked its way into the morning's more formal sessions. From the courses many friendships were created.

One Friday a guy on a course broke down in tears. Steven, a black Rastafarian, had come on in leaps and bounds in the previous two weeks and the realisation that

Monday meant a return to the real world was hard to take for him. Around 40% of those that took the course went back to work almost immediately, the percentage is still maintained to this day.

It was amazing to see how people could start building a new life in a matter of weeks. Some became self-employed; most others had joined businesses in all sorts of trades. A few years later at a Paul Weller concert, a guy came up to me and said CWB had completely transformed his life. Such moments are priceless.

Naturally there's a percentage who showed no interest in seeking work. They may be unemployed but obviously know their way around a system and how to make a few quid. One guy turned up every day in a £35K Mitsubishi. He went to all the big snooker events and was the brother of a successful player. He just wasn't interested. There is no helping some people, although that should never mean you don't try. All sorts came through the door. Not everyone wanted, or could achieve, full-time employment.

Of course, such courses don't solve all problems. They only last a few weeks at most and, in the end, it will always be up to the individuals to act on the support they're given. But these schemes can play a part.

Warwickshire were to benefit from the scheme too. Not only did the courses result in their new indoor school being booked out - business was very slow at first - but it also helped the club fulfill the terms of their funding agreements. The Edgbaston Cricket Centre was part-funded by National Lottery money; it had to be used as an asset to the community as a whole.

At the same time I wanted to deal with the roots of the problem. It was all very well treating the damaged and badly broken, but prevention is always better than cure. To this end I set up a series of coaching courses in a dozen inner city schools. The scheme, in partnership with a local funding foundation and Coachright, was often supervised by individuals who'd earned qualifications and presence through CWB; they were immediately able to pass on their new skills, confidence and drive.

In addition, schools took part in a two-day festival at a local sports club. The idea brought about the renewal of schools competing in sport. The ending of competitive sport within schools in the 80s had proved to be a very poor decision. If you don't know how to compete by the time you leave school, you'll sink before you know what's happened. Overall the cost was 68 pence per hour, per child. Interestingly enough, the team that won the organised competition was the group who beforehand lacked confidence at the thought of competing against others. The victory experience taught them a lot.

The scheme was such a success that, in time, 200 schools took part in our varied, yet cricket-based, activity, some with 'key skills' accreditation. New coaches were required all the time; activities were also run away from Edgbaston, in areas such as Handsworth, where gun and drug problems are rife. These were areas where such schemes hadn't been sustained before.

In Bristol a similar initiative was rolled out, offering Gloucestershire community coaches greater opportunities within schools, youth and cricket clubs. English cricket chief David Graveney kindly gave up his time to come and support our press day for the opening of this joint venture. The newly qualified coaches could now run courses in their own territories, not just inspiring kids to improve their cricket skills, but to engage in more wholesome activities than will have normally been the case. We'd initially put in a more experienced coach whilst newly qualified coaches found their feet; it worked as a support mechanism.

Sometimes the harshness of the communities we set about working in was brought home to us. Between 2001 and 2003 there were 110 incidents involving guns in Birmingham. There were nine murders and 40 attempted murders using illegal firearms. Many of these incidents took place near the city centre, where, on New Year's Day 2003, Letisha Shakespeare and Charlene Ellis were murdered outside a hair salon in the Birchfield Road part of the city. They were simply in the wrong place at the wrong time; caught in the crossfire of automatic weapons as two of the city's most notorious gangs continued their bloody and pointless war.

Less than half a mile away, during a session at Newtown Community Centre, we heard a gunshot. Rushing outside, we found a young guy dying on the pavement, blood running into the gutter. All this occured within yards of the popular Barton Arms pub and the A34; one of Birmingham's busiest roads.

Another time, stopping for fuel late at night, the car was immediately surrounded by addicts wanting money to feed heroin habits. I was about half-a-mile from Edgbaston, minutes from the city centre, and a stone's throw from Lea Bank, an area where efforts to secure funding for kids had been denied. At the time there was nowhere really safe for youngsters to go.

So much more gang and street crime wasn't reported. People either don't trust, or don't like, the police, and besides, the consequences of informing can be dire within a community.

There's a sub-culture in all modern cities. There are people living there who have no relationship with society, as most usually see it. They don't identify with any career structure, with family, with education or any of the other norms. Once they've left life's rails, with any safety nets long gone, it's desperately hard to get them back. We have to stimulate kids or they'll fall victim to the dangers lurking all around; it's happening everywhere, read the papers, watch the news.

Yet it was still hard to secure funding. Although we often had a positive response to initial enquiries and money was often agreed, receiving it was another matter. I've seen brilliant work cease because funding is withdrawn. Most schemes make you reapply every six or 12 months. A lot can happen over that sort of time to youngsters, especially teenagers.

The people we were working with were used to promises, mostly broken ones. We needed to show them that not everyone was the same. They would have been completely disillusioned if we had let them down. I paid for some sessions myself. Over the three years of coaching activities I ended up paying five coaches to deliver sessions after promises were made, only for the funding body to let us down. So costs for hiring facilities sometimes also had to come out of my pocket. It was worth every penny.

A good percentage of those involved still have some affiliation with local clubs or teams, but that's really of secondary importance. The communication skills and confidence that people showed will always be more valuable than the cricketing skills they will have picked up.

All this was rewarding for me. Emotionally rather than financially, but extremely rewarding nevertheless. But there was a problem. Every day I went to work there was a shadow on my shoulder; a figure that taunted me; a part of my past that wouldn't allow me to move on.

Keith Piper's presence eventually became too much for me to bear. Piper, the man who had embarked on an affair with my daughter's mother, and who was indirectly responsible for stopping me seeing my daughter.

I saw Piper daily, but not my daughter. Instead she saw him; it was as if he stepped into my life as a replacement. He was with my partner, often in my house, obviously in my bed and unlike me, he'd be with my daughter. I attended one game at Edgbaston in which Piper played, where I heard my little girl shouting Keith's name in between each delivery. It cut like a knife and I had to leave. If individuals had wanted to bring me to my knees then this was their masterstroke. I was gutted and fraught. I don't think you ever forget such things. Separation from my daughter was painful; his presence, often smirking, just rubbed salt in a wound. It reminded me of everything lost, and continually scratched at scars that wouldn't heal. It was relentless and seemed deliberate. Things were made unsustainable. I was driven out. I had to go. As much for his sake as mine.

I remember the moment I knew. It was early one evening and my phone just wouldn't stop. Ex-partners, lawyers, friends, people offering contradictory advice and trying to hush things up. All the messages were so negative; they told of who was speaking to whom and what was being said behind my back. The most memorable message finished with, "Remember Paul, a friend stabs you in the front."

But most of all the problem was dealing with the two faces of the people who had so damaged my life and relationship with my daughter. All this was happening whilst I was having meetings with Piper's players' union, the PCA, who were knee deep in helping me. Money I should have been spending on my kids was going into legal hands. I don't hate Keith Piper for this, but I hope he never has to experience such nonsense in his own life.

In the end I felt as if the only communication I received was based around requests for money. I was being hammered with demands by the Child Support Agency (CSA). On one occasion I sat in a meeting with my advisor where a figure of £56,000 was bandied about. For some time they were asking me to pay maintenance for my daughter when she was still living with me. It was madness.

Financially I was ok until I had to start defending myself. There was a fortune wasted on lawyers. It's worth noting that a recent report concluded that the CSA used 70% of what they collected from fathers just to fund their own operation. These people couldn't even program their multi-million pound computer system. It has now been recognised that they are not worth the money they consume, but I'm not sure the devastating effect they had in many lives is fully appreciated. Frankly, they were a disgrace.

My own experience of the CSA is nothing but negative. It was unsettling, costly and divisive. Often they'd lost files or letters only to make assessments based on "projected earnings" that bore no comparison to reality. This plus a sinister side, where you feel they were working against you. Effectively it feels as if these people are trying to fleece you. I thought their purpose was to chase absent fathers, not ones being torn apart from loved ones.

Personally I couldn't deal with it. Losing children is hard. The pain doesn't disappear. And when it's allied with bitterness and the financial demands of a separation it becomes difficult to take, the circumstances were absurd.

The situation wasn't ideal for a guy who had recently cleaned up after a drug problem. I had stopped taking pills before my daughter was born and knew I had turned a corner from the hole I'd dug in the mid-90s; I also knew how easy it would be to slip back into bad habits.

I've been accused of running since I took the decision to leave town. Maybe. But if I ran, I only ran in the general direction of possible work in areas I'd been successfully developing contacts over recent years. It just happened to be to Los Angeles. The problem was, at that time, I had nowhere I could stay and little money. But within a week I had spent a first night under a freeway in one of L.A.`s less glamorous suburbs. Things happened that fast.

I needed a change of scenery. A place where I wasn't judged. California offered that; I could have any day, or night, I wanted. But I was homeless. Life was full; sometimes 24-hours-a-day, you notice far more in these circumstances. You're awake a lot.

It wasn't a 100% street existence, I developed other options and sometimes I'd stay with people overnight. But if I wanted to be out under the stars I could do it. There's colder places to try it and occasionally it was liberating to do so.

If you want to see what America can be like for its homeless citizens you need to get close to observe it. Food came via fast food outlets; I had some money at the time so I was OK. I came to appreciate the 24-hour opening laws of the country. Life was scary. Often it seemed better to stay put than move about and risk bumping into problems. Other nights I'd walk through many neighborhoods.

I met some fascinating characters. Once after not eating for 36 hours I sat with a girl from Arizona in a dimly-lit, low-price cafe eating soul food. It was 4.30am. The food used the last of my cash. Later that day I phoned the UK for more money, it took three-days to get to me via a pal's home address. Over those three days I walked from one friend's address to another, it was effectively my only source of food.

I was homeless mostly through choice, and had a load of time to think about where life had to go. Improving the level of contact with my children had to be a major long-term objective. So far it is not an objective that I've been completely successful in achieving. It is, however, a long life we live.

Ultimately everything I've done from that time until now has been with that aim in mind. I knew that I had to have a sustainable business, or at least regular work. I took various qualifications and continued to gain more experience.

Really, any loss of material possessions was the least of my worries. I lost many "things". No matter. I had already lost the most important thing any parent can possess, the relationship with their children. Everything else was a detail.

On one occasion I was advised to register in England as unemployed. This at least ensured that my mortgage lender was kept at bay until a turnaround of circumstances. The episode had an immediate effect on my health, at one stage I dropped below 10 stones, a drop of 45lbs from my ideal weight when I'd played professional sport. One guy said that when I stopped messing with my body the weight would return. Ironically I had. It shows that people will always make assumptions.

In debt you learn by the hour. I felt people around me lose faith as they doubted my ability to get out of the situation. I became as broke as can be. Banks weren't interested in doing business with me in those circumstances; it felt as if there was no way out of the hole I found myself in.

If I was in England my door would constantly be knocked on by people I didn't know wanting money. Creditors asked for meetings. Fair enough. A woman's face was thunderous when she realised that one monthly outgoing from an account was for a breast implant operation. It summed up the situation. I was being fleeced and then blamed for having no money. I never even wanted the operation performed; it was another example of a person taking the piss, in this case a partner. I use that phrase loosely.

Eventually I ran out of money. I remember being in San Francisco visiting friends. Pressure was still on me to turn things around both work-wise and financially. I went to a cash machine and tried every card on me. None worked.

I was in an eight-litre Dodge Viper, about a five-hour drive from home. On the surface I must have looked quite affluent, but sometimes the things you see mask the real circumstances.

On this occasion I was alright. I had traveler's cheques on me and made it home. But there were so many debits and demands that it proved impossible to keep tabs on things. At times I'd check my accounts in the morning only to find thousands had gone by the end of the day.

In England, I recall making a car payment, then sitting down making calls and realising that by paying it, it had cleaned me out. There was no cash due for several weeks. The fridge was bare and I didn't even have money to travel to work. Ever been hungry? I don't mean missing lunch either. It is rubbish, trust me. Over the next few months I walked or caught lifts to get to work commitments. Some things just had to be postponed until another time.

All these experiences were new to me; I'd never had a cash drought before. It taught me a great deal. I never take anything for granted now. Not a roof over my head or food on the table. On occasions it felt like I was living on false promises despite my best intentions; telling people things would be alright, but not sure if I believed it any more myself. I defy anyone to retain self-confidence in the circumstances.

It's because of these sorts of problems that Fathers 4 Justice have proved important. They have highlighted the injustices that many fathers in a position similar to mine have felt; they've started to change public perceptions - and it's been a very high profile campaign.

I received a call from F4J out of the blue. I had various conversations with activists who helped organise the scaling of the walls of Buckingham Place or the throwing of flour in the House of Commons. I recall sitting on the banks of the Thames watching F4J closing London Bridge after "Spiderman" climbed to the top. The act blocked parts of the capital for three days. Watching this visual revolt strengthened my resolve, however. It made me realise that I wasn't the only one living through such predicaments and that there was some hope for the future.

Surrey and England cricketer Graham Thorpe also developed some sympathy for the F4J cause. He had huge problems trying to see the kids born from his first marriage, a situation which affected him personally and professionally. I felt for him, but I wonder what he would have felt given my circumstances, if a trusted team-mate had played a part in the breakdown of the relationship and was part of a barrier keeping him from his children?

The possibility of staging some sort of protest at a cricket match was discussed, though never seriously. Edgbaston, in central Birmingham, is a ground that regularly hosts over 20,000 spectators at televised games. I'm told it would have been easy to utilise that sort of coverage for F4J`s ends.

I didn't want to get involved. Perhaps selfishly, I couldn't see any potential improvement in my own situation if I became embroiled. Besides, it is one thing to target political figures and quite another to spoil the day for thousands of sports lovers. I still firmly believe in what Fathers 4 Justice are trying to achieve, however.

All the turmoil in my family life made my rehabilitation much harder and longer. It surely wasn't ideal for my children, either. It taught me a great deal about the importance of perception. I knew I had changed and wanted only positive results, but it suited other people to suggest that I was still out of control. I think people just thought it was easier to take sides with Piper because he was still employed by Warwickshire.

I noticed attitudes change towards me. A lot of what I thought were friendships turned out not to be. This was the second time it had happened in six years. It's chastening and it changes you as a person. I'm a wiser, but harder, man now. It had to be that way.

When I came back to England it was as if I had to start again. I hadn't been written into the evolving structure of

Cricket Without Boundaries and simply became detached from it. In retrospect I suppose that was a touch naive. I should have installed myself as a director and creamed off a percentage of the profits. Instead I allowed other people to do that. That's not meant to sound bitter; they did the right thing. The pragmatic thing. There's nothing wrong with earning a living.

It was never supposed to be about that, though. I hadn't thought about it simply as a profit-making scheme. The idea had always been to help those people who had fallen on hard times using cricket as a tool. Sure, I had wanted to carve a niche for myself too, but my own financial motivations were never the priority. If I had my time again, however, I might do things slightly differently.

Anyway, the way Cricket Without Boundaries was structured meant that as soon as I left I had no share in its profits and no way back, even to coach or mentor. What I did have was the knowledge that my ideas had proven sound and that I had made a positive difference in many lives. I'm delighted that it continues to thrive. That means a great deal to me. But it doesn't pay any bills.

The Professional Cricketers' Association helped with an introduction to The Prince's Trust. The idea was similar to Cricket Without Boundaries, but aimed more at young people between school leaving age and their mid-twenties who were in what can perhaps best be described as their vulnerable years. Usually, if kids are going to get into trouble, that's the time. My background in coaching and as the instigator of Cricket Without Boundaries was obviously advantageous; many of the aims of The Prince's Trust were identical: enhanced confidence, qualifications and a way into the job market.

The experience of homelessness in America was also vital. Many of these kids lived in hostels and often they were fascinated by tales of life in places like Compton and South Central. I have seen the results of drive-by shootings and robberies and I can impart my experiences to them. My message to these kids is that there is nothing glamorous about dying in the gutter; there is nothing glamorous about drugs, crime and violence. There is nothing glamorous about being unemployed and having no money.

It is so important to listen to what these youngsters want. It is essential for them to discover a sustainable and realistic path through life. The three rules are:

1.   It has to pay off
2.   Attend when required.
3.   Don't bring police to the door

Prince Charles actually attended a session I ran at Edgbaston. It meant a lot. It made me think back over all the work I had done since my playing career had come to a premature end and reminded me that it has not been wasted time.

I was impressed with the Prince. For over three decades this man has rallied the troops to help youngsters progress; he doesn't have to do it and he certainly doesn't have to work as hard as he does. Both he and Camilla spent quite a lot of time talking to the kids and she asked me to show her how to ball-tamper. He didn't have a bad eye for a ball either. During a brief demonstration knock against England bowlers Sajid Mahmood and Ashley Giles, he hit the latter's spin bowling for three boundaries' in four deliveries.

Even more impressive was the manner in which the kids dealt with the session. They were nerveless despite being in the presence of royalty, top cricketers and the media. They just breezed through it, telling everyone that the courses had helped them gain in confidence on their way back into work. These courses don't try and change their characters - I like the fact they all have a bit of atti-tude; a bit of spirit - but they do try to give their lives some structure and some renewed purpose. Its success rate is excellent: nearly two-thirds of those who have gone on the 12-week course go back into education or work. It's made a real difference.

Travelling around England and working with kids has been a thrill. It's rewarding to see a sullen teenager blossom with enthusiasm. So often all they need is some encouragement and support. People call this sort of work "life skills". Personally I believe it's simply a case of asking the right questions of people who normally have little attention paid to them and then taking it forward from there.

Sometimes the impact on the kids was dramatic. I remember one particular lad in Birmingham who suffered from a terrible stutter in the classroom, but who lost it completely when we were playing cricket. His confidence grew rapidly and before long he was asking me to set a bowling machine to a great pace and fire balls down at him. I believe that the confidence he gained by combating his fear of the hard ball made him focus. The result was that he spoke perfect, unbroken English for the first time in his life. People around, who'd known him for a long time, were shocked, but I'm not sure they should have been. Confidence and purpose are two of the key ingredients you need in life. It doesn't necessarily matter how you gain them, it is just important that they are present.

Smile Like You Mean It

I WAS DESTINED to be a cricketer. Both my elder brothers played for Warwickshire. David (KD Smith) left the family home in Newcastle-upon-Tyne when I was just eight years of age and went on to open the batting with Dennis Amiss. My middle brother, Tony (RA Smith), also graduated to Edgbaston when I was 12, though any chance of a career was to be ruined when a hit-and-run driver knocked him down on a zebra crossing outside the ground; a cruel blow. To make matters worse, it was the second time he had been seriously injured in such fashion. He and South African Anton Ferreira had earlier been hit by a car in a Birmingham pub car park. The guilty vehicle, a Corvette, had continued onwards, ploughing into my brother's car before accelerating up the road. Tony really didn't have much luck. Anyway, it was inevitable that I would follow my brothers to Warwickshire. They were always going to be my team.

I owe my mum and dad a great deal. My father, Ken, was an excellent communicator and had played cricket to a good standard himself. Not only did he represent Leicestershire in county cricket, but he also played with the likes of Fred Trueman during his time in the forces. But what helped all three of us was that Dad was a fine coach, who spent a lot of time helping me and my brothers develop our game.

His father had even died when playing the game. He was only 44 and batting in a village game when he was struck in the groin and collapsed. The blow precipitated a heart attack and he died immediately; a pretty harrowing experience for my nine-year-old father, who watched the whole episode from the boundary.

The incident was to have further repercussions. The family had been very well off, but with the breadwinner gone, the big home and family car soon disappeared. My father left home early to join the RAF and the rest of the family moved to more modest surroundings. Last time I checked, my family's old house was the home to Alan Milburn, the former Secretary of State for Health and MP for Darlington.

MOM & DAD

Seen here in their 30s, this pair were brilliant at encouraging me to reach for the stars. They did a fantastic job bringing up all three of their kids. My dad was the best judge of character I ever met. In many ways I wish I'd listened to him more. That was difficult after I'd left home at 16. Not long before he died my dad said to me that if Warwickshire was in Newcastle my life would have been different. In order for me to follow the professional sporting path I had to leave close friends behind and I was out on my own. Direct and important support mechanisms faded into the distance. Dad played a high level of sport himself. During his early years back in the North East he was joint professional at Ashington with West Indian Rohan Khanhai. Between the pair of them they scored bucket-loads of runs. Ashington has recently been put on the map by England fast bowler Steve Harmison - he loves the place so much he pines for it whilst touring overseas.

So cricket was in my blood; it was always going to be my destiny. Besides, there didn't seem to be too many other attractive options when looking at prospective careers. I spent much of my time at school with the attitude that this was something I had to get through; not the last time I've felt like that. One geography teacher wrote in a school report that I would never become a professional cricketer as I never focused long enough on anything to learn. Probably one or two coaches would agree with him.

That was also the attitude of my 'careers advisor' at school. Upon telling him that I wanted to be a professional cricketer he sighed and handed me some leaflets on alternative 'opportunities'. I didn't even look at them.

It's probably fair to say my old school, Heaton, at this stage wouldn't have topped too many league tables, had they existed. On one occasion it made the national news after riots broke out following the school's decision to impose the same punishments - including the cane - on boys and girls. Riot police with dogs had to be called to save teachers from being beaten up by a crowd of around 600 irate pupils and their parents. One teacher actually came close to being lynched. He was beaten up pretty badly by the mob before escaping to safety. By the time police dispersed the throng, there was hardly a window in the school that hadn't been smashed.

Nor was it an open-minded environment. I recall being told to "watch who I was hanging around with" after befriending a boy from China, while when a little girl from the Sudan joined our class the teacher asked her "which tribe" she came from.

There was not a great deal of sport played at the school. The older kids went on strike early in my school career, refusing to represent the establishment, while I remember PE lessons more as an opportunity to make fun than anything else. About the only thing I remember about school sport from the period was our PE teacher - Mr Taylor - impaling himself on a trampoline as he tried to demonstrate the right technique. The whole class burst into laughter as he rolled around in agony. Our "inhuman lack of action" sentenced us to several weeks of cross country runs as punishment.

It says a lot for the ingenuity of the people in the area that so many ex-pupils have gone on to lead successful careers in such diverse fields. One of my best friends from school days is Simon Donald, who went on to form the comic Viz with his brother Chris. Simon was always funny; always full of artistic talent. Like me he spent a considerable amount of his early life playing pranks, often in school time when we had our biggest audience. He was told on more than one occasion that wit and cartoon drawing would get him nowhere. I have clear memories of helping sell the first edition of *Viz* at the Gosforth Hotel. Every copy sold out on the first evening. The following weekend we sold it in Newcastle city centre with similar results. It's proved to be a huge success.

"Smile like you mean it" was a phrase snapped at me by a teacher. It's funny how things stick in your mind. They must have spent hours telling me the dates of battles and the capital cities of various countries, but that's the phrase that stayed with me. As I've grown up it's helped me identify what are those moments of true happiness - fleeting and transitory though they might be - as opposed to those when you feel you have to turn on a false smile like you would a tap. I'm not saying you should judge someone by their smile, but it is a fair indicator of their personality.

One day at school a disagreement occurred between a female classmate and a staff teacher, who unfortunately sported a walrus-style moustache. Listening, the class burst into laughter after he suggested our classmate was "immature". She replied: "How man, raggy tash? Don't call me immature, I've had more cocks than you've had hot dinners!" That pretty much sums things up.

At this age I went on my first cricket tour with the nomadic Vikings cricket club. It has been said that I spent the next 20 years living as if I was on tour. I immediately took to the freedom of a life away from home. I thrived on the hotel living and travel and soon realised that if cricket could help me do this and meet a host of interesting new

EARLIEST PRESS PIC - AGED 13

Even at this age I knew I would play this sport for a job - every minute I was somewhere playing or practicing it. In a Geography class I sat and looked at a world map, picking out countries I wanted to see, a feat I managed to achieve many times. It proved the biggest education of any thing. At school Simon Donald was forever being told that drawing cartoons would not give him any start in life - proven wrong when Virgin boss Richard Branson started offering massive cheques to him later on.
Me, I was told to stop looking out of the school windows at our playing fields. Once I was sent to a visiting careers advisor who looked blankly at me when I replied I'd play cricket for a living, I was given a million leaflets about careers which simply didn't interest me and sent back out.

people, then it was the life for me. With no home ground, we spent nearly every Sunday traveling to distant villages and taking on the locals. The Vikings team played a big part in my formative years.

Cricket was an escape from the hardship of life that I saw around me. I soon realised that being good at the game afforded me opportunities that many other people of my age didn't have.

A clear example of that came to me when I was a 15 year-old. I spent a weekend with my future Warwickshire team-mates when they were on a Rohan Kanhai benefit trip to the north east of the country. Rohan had been a fellow professional with my father at Ashington years before and had then gone on to lead the West Indies to World Cup glory and play for many years with much success for Warwickshire. There was good camaraderie between the different groups of people involved.

Anyway, as part of the trip I met a woman outside a pub. It was the moment that I realised that paid performers were treated differently. I'm sure she wouldn't have extended the same favours to any 15 year-old boy and I soon developed a taste for the treatment. Sport: it obviously carried with it other advantages and offerings.

One guy who made an impression on me at that time of life was Newcastle United's Malcolm MacDonald. A group of us watched him score five goals for England versus Cyprus at Wembley. A few weeks afterwards I saw 'Super Mac' climb out of a gold Ferrari outside St. James' Park. Later on he appeared as a competitor on the TV show *Superstars* and ran the 100 meters in a time of 10.4 seconds, which made him the third fastest sprinter in the UK. He could have gone to the Olympics!

In an area where money was tight and life sometimes seemed very hard, such a lifestyle was enormously attractive. My life so far had been easier than some, yet I knew sport as a profession was my best option. It certainly inspired me to perform on bigger stages and build a life for myself away from pits, shipyard or factory.

Much later in life I appeared on a TV show with Super Mac and Simon Donald. By now Macdonald was married to the ex-wife of AC/DC lead singer Brian Johnson. Johnson himself had lived in a house overlooking Heaton School and some days we would see him riding a Harley-Davidson past the school gates. To a young and impressionable boy who didn't see much of a future for himself in the traditional job market, such characters showed what could be achieved by backing yourself and following the path less travelled.

At around this time in my life Bob Willis made a first visit to my family home. I had only ever seen him on TV. Sometimes my brother spoke of games the two had played in and how Willis had bowled. He certainly left an impression

AGED 13 AT JESMOND

First press photo call on my home ground. By the age of 13, I'd regularly struck opposing bowlers out of this ground. Not many did that, not at any age. During summer school break I was made to run round the ground's perimeter by a visiting coach as punishment for playing positive shots to deliveries he wanted me to defend. The fact the balls went for 4s & 6s went unrecognised. I was lucky - I knew my dad was a better coach and communicator - to some, this idiot would be their introduction to being coached.

and meeting him as a kid inspired me to want to play where he did. His belief that I should have played Test Match and One-Day International cricket for England still means a great deal to me.

During my early visits to Birmingham I would spend every spare moment watching the cricket. Sitting in a packed Edgbaston watching a one-day game I recall Indian international spinner, Dilip Doshi, struggling in the field. One supporter shouted to Warwickshire's captain, "Give him a fucking skateboard, Willis" as another ball eluded Dilip's grasp. I laughed along with the rest, but I do remember thinking that such a profession in the public eye did leave players open to terrible abuse and criticism from the spectators. Still, I knew before I became a pro that Edgbaston was where I wanted to ply my trade.

Later, in my own debut season, I witnessed Gladstone Small bowl a 19-ball over; 12 no-balls and a wide as Australian umpire Bill Alley called "no ball" time and time again. Our Bajan eventually delivered the ball off a two-pace run up, only to hear the umpire shout "wide". By the time the over was concluded, a clearly distressed bowler took his sweater and walked down to the boundary, receiving catcalls and abuse. "Bloody rubbish, Small," shouted one spectator. "Crap," cried another. And all this at a home game! These were our supporters. It was the first time I'd witnessed this type of reaction from fans directed at a team-mate. It shocked me. And Gladstone. Cricket has always been a much easier game to play from the stands than on the pitch.

Sometimes the spectators simply don't understand what is going on. During the 1995 season Andy Moles received some fearful stick from the crowd after two plates of sandwiches were delivered for him while he was batting. Moles was always on the rotund side and it must have appeared as if he were just a bloater who couldn't wait for his next meal. Actually, however, he had recently been diagnosed as diabetic and needed to keep a close eye on his blood sugar levels. In the circumstances he did very well to have such a successful career as a sportsman. Personally I think he should have opened the batting for England. Many lesser players did.

Anyway, sometime after that first taste of life at Edgbaston the letter I had been longing for arrived through

THE WARWICKSHIRE COUNTY CRICKET CLUB

[Letterhead with club administration details]

4th January, 1982.

Mr. P. Smith,
13, Bull Street,
Harborne,
Birmingham 17.

Dear Paul,

Contract Terms, Season 1982.

When my Committee met the other day they decided upon Players' salaries for 1982. In consequence they have instructed me to write to you saying that for the season they would propose to pay you a basic salary of £1800. In addition, there will, of course, be the usual kind of bonuses, though these have yet to be precisely agreed.

I look forward to receiving a note from you as soon as possible to say that these terms are acceptable.

May I take the opportunity of wishing you a very happy and successful 1982.

Yours sincerely,

Alan C. Smith,
General Secretary.

FIRST CONTRACT

Obviously it's a happy day when that letter finally arrives. Confirmation at last that your dreams of being a professional sportsman are to be realised.

Clubs play on those hopes, however. This wonderfully vague letter from Warwickshire CCC states that I'll be paid "the usual type of bonuses." No details, just a request for me to accept!

The one from the MCC which fell through my letter box offering me terms on their groundstaff stated: "I regret that it is not possible to let you have an Agreement for signature, but the terms and conditions of employment will be outlined... at the trial."

The Professional Cricketers' Association - and the professionalism of some agents - have done much to make the relationship make more equal these days, but for far too long clubs had it their own way. Players were poorly paid and poorly looked after. To call first-class cricket a professional sport was at times merely a figure of speech.

my door. It was a month after my 16th birthday. It contained the dates of my trial period at Warwickshire and included the address of the hotel and the playing and practice itinerary. This was it. I read it in front of my father and went off to school.

On the short walk I had all sorts of conflicting emotions going through my head, however. The very first game of my Warwickshire trial coincided with a planned meeting with American rock guitarist Ted Nugent, to take place in Newcastle. For ages I'd followed this guy's success across the other side of the ocean. A meeting had been organised for months through a connection. I knew my dad would go nuts if he knew I was even considering not attending the trial. All day I thought it over. I didn't even tell anyone at school the letter had arrived.

AGED 15 AT JESMOND

Even at this age I could surprise my elders with pace. A slingshot-type delivery style surprised people at times and lead to wickets consistently falling in clusters. Strike rates play a massive part in cricket and are often overlooked. Out and out effort every ball takes some doing, but the rewards are there for the taking. The consistency of some of the worlds greatest who I played against used to intrigue me. For some time I was reported upon and seen as the quickest white man with a ball in his hand.

About 10 years after this pic was taken the workload had started to affect my knees, I could still bowl quick, but the down side was day after day of my body aching. I played hundreds of games, batting and bowling, on top of training on rock hard surfaces. Often the real killer was the travel. Levels of knowledge about the human body within this era varied in relation to a sportsmen. It had been predicted that my flatmate Gladstone Small would only have a short career due to being born with fewer vertebrae - he obviously proved science and experts wrong as he won 17 England Test caps and 53 in One-Day Internationals. Too many consecutive days' play led to more than running repairs. Most practice sessions took place in a netted environment - alien - it didn't resemble the space where we were expected to perform. Because of this lack of familiarity with the pitch it took longer to find form in the middle. New coach Bob Woolmer took Edgbaston groundsman Andy Atkinson to task about us being not allowed to practice on the main ground. Woolly got his way and we took down the "Atkinson's Nurseries" sign from the entrance onto the main playing area! Liverpool may have had "Welcome to Anfield", we had "Welcome to Atkinson's Nurseries"! Embarrassing really.

Later that evening I plucked up the courage to mention my dilemma to my dad. I suggested that he could ring Warwickshire for me and ask if we could arrange different dates. He was furious. Understandably, in retrospect. His response showed how much my success meant to him. Few fathers will have spent as much time with their kids as mine did. The fact I was as good at my age can be put down to him. His spirit made mine.

"It's all been done before, son," he used to tell me. Much later I realised that he was right. I once sat next to an elderly gentleman at an official function who told me a story about the female ice cream seller at Edgbaston in the 1950s who used to offer 'extras' during quiet passages of play. Many took great pleasure in her services.

I spent loads of time with my dad during my childhood. Cricket was a formality whilst things like trips to the nearby Northumberland coastline or treks into all the old haunts he roamed as a kid took place.

I was to wait nearly a decade and a half before I came across another coach who had that level of communication skills. At different times in my professional career I had coaches who thought they were doctors, dieticians, physiotherapists and my landlady.

Growing up, I would sometimes play two games a day. The first one would start at 11am and finish around 5.30 to 6. My father would then drive me to my next game. I played in many of these types of games up to near on 9pm. When I was supposed to do any homework I'm not sure. This, no doubt, is one of the reasons why I might have fallen foul of some of my teachers.

As a young professional I was keen to play as much as possible. I knew I could bowl fast and, at that stage, it was easy for me to do it as often as I liked. At the time I was playing solely for Warwickshire seconds and in the Birmingham League, so there were plenty of days when I didn't have that much to do. While out socially one weekend I bumped into friends of my brother who persuaded me to play a couple of games for their local club side. In the first game I took eight wickets and broke an opponent's arm. I had to be escorted off the pitch at the end of play by a debt collector who was a team-mate on the day. My intimidating bowling seemingly made the opposition irate.

The second fixture was a national knockout game. The competition rules stated that no professionals were allowed to partake, so it was agreed that I would play under the name of Jim Morrison; a reference to the lead singer of The Doors. Again I did pretty well and helped the team to victory. The following Friday's headline in the local weekly paper was, "Jim opens the Doors for Solihull". Priceless.

The physical strain on a young body playing so much is now well documented. These days a player aged under 17 is not allowed to deliver more than three bowling spells in a day. I often wonder if it played a part in me having knee problems later in my career.

One of the first things I learned was the fragile nature of the profession. A sporting career can end in a moment. Watching Andy Lloyd's Test debut against the West Indies in 1984 was a case in point: my Warwickshire colleague had batted brilliantly for several seasons and thoroughly deserved his call-up. Yet on his very first morning of Test cricket he found himself batting against one of the most fearsome pace attacks of all time and taking a horrible blow on the eye socket from a Malcolm Marshall delivery. It was a long way back for Andy; indeed he was never the same as a batsman. He was told by doctors that he was lucky just to survive.

As a kid I once went with my father to watch Warwickshire take on Yorkshire at Bradford. As my brother walked out to bat, the local crowd were whipped into a fury merely by his partner Amiss wearing a protective batting helmet. From close quarters I watched as the pair were actually jostled by the local crowd. I bet most of those Yorkshire supporters would have been wearing one if they had had to bat. As if to prove the point, later in the month I sat at Trent Bridge as Warwickshire played Nottinghamshire. I witnessed my brother being stretchered off the pitch having been struck on his unprotected left temple by a short fast delivery from South African Clive Rice. A crack sound echoed around the ground. Really, he was lucky to escape with his life. I sat in the main stand shocked as he was carried off unconscious. It made me even more angry with that crowd at Bradford who appeared so aggrieved at protective helmets being worn out there.

I sustained pretty unpleasant facial injuries myself after batting against Courtney Walsh a few years later in 1989. I had made the mistake of irritating the West Indian fast bowler - once the world record holder for the number of Test wickets taken - during a one-day game the previous day, and our contest spilled over into the first-class game. I scored 61 to help us win the one-day game, with a good percentage of them coming against Walsh, who conceded over 50 from five overs. He was livid.

The following day we resumed our Championship fixture. I walked to the wicket with the game delicately poised and straightaway took four runs off the Jamaican, pulling him in front of the square leg umpire to the boundary. Soon afterwards I attempted a similar shot, only to deflect the ball into my face. Immediately there was a lot of blood and a tremendous amount of pain, but I only realised how bad it was from the look on other people's faces. It was not quite the second wedding anniversary I had planned. I remained conscious throughout; unfortunately.

I was taken to the physio's room for examination. Gladstone Small had been sleeping, but to see the horrified look on his face even made me laugh. By this stage, however, it was clear it was quite a serious injury. I lost a lot of blood and the pain was intense.

Alan Oakman drove me to hospital. "Let's have a look then," he said. He exhaled sharply. "Fuck me, Smithy," he said with feeling. "That's a bad 'un." Alan dropped me off at the hospital. "I'm off then," Oakman said; it was the end of his working day. I watched him drive away and wandered into the hospital, hardly able to see.

A surgeon wasn't available, so instead a nurse stitched the gaping hole over where my nose used to be. No sooner had she finished than her bleeper went and I was told a reconstructive surgeon was available and could operate immediately - but at a nearby hospital. The only problem was that it meant those stitches had to be undone again. Fortunately the surgeon went to work soon afterwards and I was released into unconsciousness.

The morning wasn't so good, though. I awoke in a ward with yards of tissue up both nostrils and a metal plate and hinge where my forehead and nose used to be. They are still there. Later on the surgeon told me the damage was as bad as a serious car accident. He reckoned the ball hit me at well over 100m.p.h.

Courtney, being the good fellow that he is, called and offered to pay for the surgery. I declined the offer; it's all part of the game. He didn't mean to hurt me; he was just doing the job of the damn fine fast bowler that he was.

Soon afterwards I was taken home. I was under strict instructions not to move around and to avoid any pressure on the front of my head. Within minutes of reaching my house, however, my young son jumped from behind me and smashed a miniature cricket bat straight on to my face. Kids; you've got to love them! Originally I was told not to play for six months, but the club needed me and I wanted to play. Within 16 days I played for Warwickshire in a semi-final against Worcestershire. I do remember as I ran in to bowl there was an almighty crunch as the hinge and plate moved positions in my head. "What the hell was that?" Allan Donald asked me from mid-off. "Just my nose, Allan," I said.

It was damn painful, but I took three wickets, we won the game and went on to lift the Trophy, beating Middlesex in the final. I was forced to take a break from playing over the winter, however, which meant I couldn't take up the offer to play as a professional for The University of Western Australia that winter. I suffered from terrible headaches for months afterwards and decided the best thing was to rest over the winter.

It could have been worse. West Indian Phil Simmons was hit on the temple by a bouncer from Gloucestershire fast bowler David 'Syd' Lawrence; it almost killed him. Simmons' heart stopped in the ambulance on his way to

THE AFTER EFFECTS OF BEING HIT AT SPEED

The results of a Courtney Walsh bouncer. I top-edged my shot and broke several bones in my face. Smarted a bit. I'm often asked what it's like to face quick bowlers. People in America simply don't understand. I tell them to imagine the fastest baseball pitcher flinging a ball straight at your temple at 90 plus mph; and then imagine that somehow you've survived. It takes as little as 0.3 seconds before the ball is upon you when the fastest are firing on all cylinders. These guys are often relentless in charging in again and again to bowl directly at you, only next time there's a chance it'll be directed straight at your ankle, groin or throat.

In many ways baseball hitters have it easy. The pitcher throws directly in a striker's arc. If the pitcher throws straight at an opponent's body then there's hell to pay. Often it'll end in a fight. Not in cricket. If that kind of damage occured in everyday life you'd call the police.

As a cricketer you expect to get struck occasionally. It doesn't matter what stage of your career you're at. It's damn hard, especially as, often, you'll be fatigued. In this picture you clearly see the end result when things go against you. The pain of this blow really was horrific. Several months later I was still suffering headaches and blurred vision.

Earlier in my career I sat at a Test Match in the Caribbean in the stands with local supporters watching as Michael Holding terrorised batsmen with his pace. A Rasta stood a few feet away, a massive reefer in one hand and a bottle of the local brew in the other. He repeatedly shouted, "Lick 'im, Mikey," as each 95mph delivery flew at his opponent. One thing was for sure, if our Rasta friend faced Mikey after smoking half of what was in his hand, you'd pay to see it.

hospital and he required brain surgery. Graeme Watson's injury was even worse. He required 40 pints of blood and heart massage to recover after he was struck down by a Tony Greig beamer.

As a boy I remember being unimpressed when Bishan Bedi declared his Indian team's second innings with only half the side dismissed in a Test against the West Indies in 1975. He wasn't willing to let his other players face such brutal fast bowling. He had already seen two of his batsmen retire hurt earlier in proceedings. In retrospect, I understand what he meant. It's dangerous out there. And in the days before helmets it was lethal. If you've never faced the fastest then don't even comment.

Not everyone can pretend to be brave. When we played a game against Middlesex early in my career, Antiguan Tony Merrick was bowling horribly fast for us. Phil Tufnell was their last batsman and looked absolutely terrified. Somehow he survived his first ball, the last of Merrick's over, before taking an almost impossible run - and somehow making it - off the last ball of the next over to ensure he didn't have to face the paceman again. The first ball of the next over knocked his partner off his feet, but after the lbw appeal was rejected the pair could have taken an easy single. "You must be fucking joking if you think I'm going back down there," Tufnell yelled as his partner scampered down the wicket. He simply refused to run.

On another occasion during a game at Old Trafford I was struck on my left hand by a vicious delivery from Pakistani Wasim Akram. It completely shattered my knuckle on my little finger. Bloody agony. At hospital the doctor just told me to get used to being a knuckle short. He told me the fragments of the other one would pass through, and out, of my body within the week. Nice.

Playing against some of those guys was no fun at all. Walking out to bat against Hampshire one day, Malcolm Marshall sidles up to me. "Don't worry, Smithy Boy," he said. "This won't take long." He was right. After he just failed to decapitate me with his first ball, the second hit my thumb, directly in front of my eyes, as I tried to protect my head from a 90mph missile. The ball cleared the keeper and bounced twice before clattering into the advertising boards. Next ball I was dismissed. Again the ball hit my thumb, only this time it had ripped the protection and my thumb nail off on its way to the keeper.

I was on the other end of such intimidation at times. During a Birmingham League game against Walsall I was called back into the attack to finish the game off. I delivered a series of short balls directed at the batsmen's heads and upper bodies and soon had the game wrapped up. On the way off the pitch, however, I was attacked by the mother of one of the players. She kept hitting me with an umbrella and shouting "bloody hoodlum". After a few seconds of this one of her friends came up. I presumed she was going to pull her away, but instead she joined in: "You weren't playing cricket," she said. "You were trying to bloody murder."

Of course not all such career-threatening injuries are caused on the pitch. Rather like my brother, opening batsman Robin Dyer's most serious concern came when he fell off a mini-motorbike whilst going round a traffic island in wet conditions and seriously damaged his little finger. After several operations, and being obliged to wear a splint for several months, amputation was even considered!

His brother-in-law, batsman, and now Chairman of Cricket at Warwickshire, John Claughton, saw his career ended in an instant. His knee suddenly went on him when he was running between the wickets and he never played for us again; it made the blood of everyone in the dressing room run cold. He was seen as a future county captain and instead was forced out of the game in his early 20s. It could have happened to any of us at any time.

The care given to cricketers in those days was anything other than professional. Very early on in my career I watched Phil Oliver, a young batsman with more talent than most, undergo several knee operations before a second opinion identified that it was his hip that was the cause of his problems. By that time his dream career was gone. My own brother David had a big shoulder operation at the end of one season. Four months later the scar burst open while he lay on a beach whilst he was on honeymoon. Luckily his wife was a nurse. He had to wear sanitary towels over the wound until they returned to the UK.

There were a couple of times when I feared my career might be over almost before it had started. In my first season as a professional I suffered a stress fracture of my back and was put in plaster from below my waist to my upper chest. At the time I was told I'd have to wear it for up to six months! It was unbearable; they were to prove the longest months of my life. Watching the other guys play wasn't easy. With nothing to do and no physiotherapy requirements, I felt like a spare part around players.

It was an odd period. To some extent I had everything I wanted. I was a professional cricketer and living in one of the houses located actually within the famous Edgbaston ground that had fascinated me for years. In other ways, however, I was as far away from fulfilling my dream as ever. My career was in real jeopardy.

I climbed out of bed one morning and jumped in the shower with my music booming. It must have been really loud for, 90 metres away, it caused the first-class game to be stopped. Bob Willis apparently said that he couldn't concentrate! I reckon he would have been fine if it had been Bob Dylan's music blaring out across the stadium. Anyway, it took some time before someone came into the house and turned the music down. I was still in the shower.

Willis spoke to me about the incident afterwards. Although he told me not to do it again, he was fine. I think he understood. I was a young guy worried that my career was fading away while the world went on and perhaps, subconsciously, the incident was a manifestation of my desire to be the centre of attention.

After another frustrating visit to the specialist I took matters into my own hands. I sat in a bath armed with a kitchen knife and cut through my cast until I could tear if off. It felt like the weight of the world had been lifted off my shoulders. Within minutes I joined the other players in a local pub. I felt like a new man.

Unfortunately it never takes long for word to get around a dressing room. The next morning I was summoned into the club to provide an explanation, then sent straight back to the hospital for a new cast to be fitted. The bollocking I received wasn't the worst, but my lack of professionalism was noted. A few months later my cast was finally removed. I was allowed to resume gentle training and, before long, I was selected to play in a reserve fixture on a beautifully fast and bouncy wicket. The temptation to bowl proved too much; I knew I could bowl fast by this age and was naive enough to be swayed into trying. Disaster struck almost immediately, shooting pains returned to my back and legs. Within a few hours of thinking my season was relaunched I was heading back to hospital. It effectively ended my season.

Another incident of note from this first summer involved one of my housemates. Kassem Ibadulla would receive a hard punch towards the top of his right arm every morning in the changing rooms before play from ex-miner Chris Lethbridge. Often it led to Kassem suffering a dead arm and being unable to bowl. Many times Kassem asked Chris why he did It. Lethbridge would simply reply, "Because I can." Kassem couldn't win. His father, Billy, a Warwickshire stalwart, was actually living with us at the time whilst carrying out his duties as a first-class umpire. One night Billy returned home late after a long drive. It was midnight and I was lying in bed, listening as the car pulled up and he climbed the stairs. Soon there was a huge crash as he sat on his bed and it broke in two. Chris had actually sawn the bed frame in two, a prank he clearly aimed at Kassem. I denied all knowledge.

It took a while for me to regain full fitness. The key was the chance to winter in Johannesburg after winning a Warwickshire scholarship. I returned fitter, stronger and quicker than ever.

During that winter I worked under the management of Dr. Ali Bacher. The West Rand based side that Bacher had asked me to represent during my stay proved a fun-loving bunch, and was captained by Ali`s number two, Ashley

Harvey-Walker. Ashley was only recently retired from English professional cricket at Derbyshire and was still more than capable of scoring runs when others didn't. Our Florida team also had future South African International Brian McMillan within it. Mac had yet to really show the sort of promise that would elevate him into the brilliant Transvaal side and his path at that time was blocked by our fellow team-mate Francois Weiderman, who was just starting to make an impact with the Transvaal XI, nicknamed the 'dream team'. I went out with François's beautiful sister during my stay.

Brian Mac sold his wicket hard. He loved occupying the crease. Anyone who verballed him did so at their peril; he was as hard as nails, even as a teenager. All Mac ever needed to reply was, "What's that, China?" Any aggravation disappeared.

Later he joined us for a season at Warwickshire. Once some guys tried to mug us late at night on Harborne high street in Birmingham. They couldn't have picked a worse guy to target. His response was quick and vicious; much like his bowling.

I would see Bacher every day at the Wanderers. He was driven in his quest for multi-cultural cricket and encouraged us to sell our sport to as many kids as possible. We taught in Soweto and Alexandria and all sorts of other townships around Jo'burg. I had never seen deprivation like it. The living conditions were simply inhumane; it was clear that treating people like this was storing up trouble for the future. These people were disadvantaged from the moment they were born. They had little education and greatly reduced life expectancy. They didn't have much hope. For a young white boy who had done nothing but play cricket, it was a life-altering experience; more educational than many years at Heaton.

There was wonderful enthusiasm for our work, however. Whenever we took the kit into the townships kids would run to play in their masses. The results were excellent. People of all backgrounds, faiths and colours would play together and learn that there were many more similarities

AGED 18 COACHING IN JOHANNESBURG

*In amongst others are the children of Alvin Kallicharan and Dr Ali Bacher - at this
time the most important figures in my sport in this country. South Africa was still
living under Apartheid and Johannesburg was an unusually aggressive place. Ashley
Harvey Walker, seen here on the extreme left, later had his head blown off by a
shot gun in a Hilbrow club he owned. It was a venue where we spent much time.
The type of coaching session shown here often took us into Soweto, Alexandria
and other townships circling Jo'burg. They were rough places where anything could
happen. Later in life I worked in similar places in the Cape. The Cape Flats are
thought to house around 10 million unregistered guns.*

than differences between them. Bridges between communities were built and, in time, it played a part in stopping people of different colours fighting each other.

Bacher was the key implementer for this work. He drove himself on through long days and nights at the Wanderers Stadium office, all this despite a recently completed heart bypass operation. Often I would go running with him at midday. Johannesburg is 6,000 feet above sea level and under an African sun it could be desperately hard work. I had been told he had been an inspirational leader of the South African side; it wasn't hard to see why. He was an inspiring man and the work inspired much of what I was to do later.

Sometimes I had the impression that he didn't necessarily approve of my lifestyle, however. One day he gave me a prescription and asked me to take it to a chemist.

When I brought the bottles of pills back to him he said they were actually all for me. "They'll make you calm down, Paul," he said. Nice try, but I ask any 18 year-old let loose in Johannesburg to live a quiet existence. I think Bacher understood that.

During one of the unofficial 'Rebel' Tests against a touring West Indies side - South Africa was still morbidly in the grip of Apartheid at the time - I was charged with selling memorabilia from a caravan behind the Wanderers stadium changing rooms with Richard Ellison. With one of the bowlers on a hat-trick I was lured away from my post to watch the action and sprinted down to see what was to happen. Within a minute we had sprinted back to duty; but too late. We found that every item in the caravan had been swiped. We tried to work out what to say to Ali. Thankfully South Africa had enjoyed a good day at the office. He laughed and told us to be a bit more careful next time.

One night I was invited to a cocktail party at Johannesburg's most prestigious hotel in the centre of town. I met the Roxy Music singer Brian Ferry there and enjoyed a discussion about our upbringings in the north of England. Whilst in his company I glanced down to see that he had no shoes or socks on, despite it being a black tie event. He was still easily the coolest guy in the room.

Sadly the many fond memories I retain of this time are tainted by sadness. Both Francois and Harvey-Walker have since been murdered in South Africa. It's a shock to the system when people you know well die in violent circumstances. Johannesburg, in particular, has become much more violent. There is a great deal of anger and poverty and there are parts of the place where it is simply just foolish to visit. The last time I was in Hilbrow a young black South African stood wearing a 2Pac t-shirt, looking people up and down, daring them to look him in the eye. His clothes were the same colour as those worn by Crip gang members in Los Angeles; it reminded me that American gang culture had arrived in South Africa some time back. It made me think that the imagery sold by the American music industry had worked.

IN JOHANNESBURG WITH ENGLAND'S RICHARD ELLISON

The two of us spent six months in and around the Wanderers Stadium, practising and playing with some of the world's top performers. I learnt more in this period than in years talking to manual-toting coaches back in England. I wish I had spent longer there; it might have made all the difference. In this picture we're selling memorabilia for the 'rebel' West Indies tour of the Republic. About half-an-hour after the picture was taken we took our eyes off the stall only to find that every single thing was stolen.

A few summers later I recall standing with Elly out in the middle on his home ground at Canterbury. He had just been called up by the England selectors and was about to depart for Edgbaston to play against Australia in the fifth Test. I wished him luck and hoped he had the rub of the green.

That game saw Ian Botham hit his first and third deliveries for towering sixes. There was also a flash flood which turned everything for miles around into a lake. And "Rilla" Ellison took 4 wickets in a 15 ball spell. I stood with Beefy`s manager Tim Hudson watching events unfold. During this Test match Rich took 10 Australian wickets and received the man of the match award. I was delighted for him. When it was his day, and conditions suited, he could be a nightmare to face. In this picture we appear blurry eyed. It may have had some thing to do with Ashley Harvey Walker, a bottle of Cane, and most definitely, brandy and coke. Over these 6 months Rich and I shared a sponsored car and, in those pre-mobile phone days, he was often unable to trace my whereabouts. I know I drove him nuts on occasions when he was waiting for me to return with the keys.

I just wish the killers of my friends and team-mates had known how much this pair had done to try to help people living in their townships. They did everything they could to improve life for black youngsters by playing and coaching kids. Their reward? Harvey-Walker had his head blown off one night in his own bar and Francois was shot repeatedly as he climbed out of his car at a golf course.

It was always a violent place. Once during a Friday night party in Hilbrow a neighbour aimed his AK47 across high-rise balconies in our direction because no one would turn down music that he deemed to be too loud.

On another occasion I was awoken in the early hours by a large bang from three stories below. A black guy had ploughed his car into mine at the side of the road. Within minutes four police officers had sprayed gas into his eyes and were handing out a vicious baton attack as he lay by the side of the road, trying unsuccessfully to defend himself. It resembled everything witnessed in the Rodney King case. This was 1983 and the murder of Steve Biko whilst in police custody in Port Elizabeth in 1977 was still fresh in the mind. The atrocity highlighted what was happening in the country.

The townships of the 80s were like nothing I had ever seen. Guns were everywhere. There were military vehicles on most street corners and every day brought news about a 'necklacing' in the vicinity; that's where car tyres were wrapped around some unfortunate victim, doused in petrol and set alight.

At times it was frightening just traveling around. Driving on freeways you had to avoid bricks hung on ropes from bridges; they were designed to smash through car windscreens and cause crashes. In Cape Town, all the streetlights on the roads approaching the airport were shot out so that you had to drive in the dark for long distances; it made it easier to stage ambushes. It wasn't much like Northumberland at all.

The likes of Allan Donald had to serve their national service patrolling this type of area. He talked of finding dogs with their throats cut hanging from wires, their blood trails highlighted by the moon. You bet he was scared.

When I first arrived in South Africa I recall seeing a body lying in the road. Instinctively I was stopping the car when my passenger told me to speed up and drive away. I thought they were being cruel, but they quickly explained that this was a ruse designed to encourage the innocent to stop their cars and offer their help. No sooner did this happen, than 'the body' would suddenly jump up and, joined by others who were hiding nearby, would take your car. Sometimes they would also kill the occupants; sometimes they wouldn't. They didn't seem to have too much respect for human life.

On another occasion I crashed my car into a brick wall as I tried to avoid a vehicle that was trying to run me off the road. I was travelling to pick up Richard Ellison at the time and the crash meant we missed a flight we needed to take to play in Barry Richards' benefit game in Durban. Fortunately we did eventually make it; neither of us could believe we were in the same team as such greats of our sport and the floodlit game we played in was an opportunity not to be missed.

With my stay in South Africa's biggest city coming to an end I gave my maid from my apartment its entire contents, including food left on the shelves. Grace lived in Soweto and each day took two long bus journeys to work. It meant an early start for this mother of many; she'd get the bus clearly marked "BLACKS". My maid's life revolved around whatever work she could fit into any one day. When I told her she could have all appliances she replied, "Thank you, master", then burst into tears. Being called 'master' by a women three times my age never sat comfortably with me. I was obviously still learning about the history of South Africa. This lady had seen plenty in her life. She was a humble soul and could have taught the country's rulers quite a bit on the ethics of life. She inspired me during my time there.

Johannesburg was also a brilliantly instructive time in terms of learning about cricket. Each day I had the opportunity of practicing with the likes of Graham Pollock, one of the greatest ever batsmen, Jimmy Cook, Clive Rice and West Indian Sylvester Clarke. Just seeing how they went about things was eye-opening.

I tried speaking to a Warwickshire coach on my return to Edgbaston about how things were going. Was I doing the right things; how did he think I was batting and bowling? I thought it would help me keep on top of issues and learn more. These talks had been a weekly ritual in Jo`burg, yet back in England, after an uncomfortable five-minute discussion, I left the room confused and uninspired. It did not go as I had expected. Later that week I was taken aside by my older brother and told my request for a meeting had been interpreted as attention-seeking. I replied I wanted to progress and was seeking feedback. The reaction wasn't what I expected from someone who was effectively a tutor or teacher.

In England things progressed pretty well over the next few years. My only major injury problem appeared in my left knee. It had never been an issue until I was forced to do star jumps in a sports hall in Balsall Heath. There was no padding on the floors and upon landing I felt my knee give way.

To me the incident shows a fair bit about the direction that cricket has gone in recent years. I think there is far too much emphasis on fitness and not enough on skills. I also wonder if the injury problems with current players are caused by the sheer volume of fitness work they undertake. The wear and tear they put on their bodies with the shuttle runs, the twisting and turning and just the volume of work required by the joints is, in my opinion, unsustainable. I really do wonder whether Ashley Giles' hip problems and Michael Vaughan's knee problems have been caused by their bowling or batting. The amount of fitness work they have done is a key factor, I suspect.

Anyway, the incident meant that my knee would sometimes lock and resulted in greatly reduced mobility. My style of bowling was hard on my legs, with around eight times my body weight being forced through my knee each time I delivered a ball. Bowling had become easier in terms of gaining the results, but it was physically becoming harder to put as much effort into each delivery. Eventually, despite a host of conflicting advice and opinions, it was decided to operate; a big decision for a 27-year-old whose livelihood depended on the outcome.

As I sat in the private hospital, pondering an uncertain future, a woman I knew entered the room. She was the best friend of a playing colleague's wife. And she was the nurse charged with implanting suppositories up my back-side; a pretty awkward situation bearing in mind I often saw her in social situations. In fact, I've often wondered what she is thinking when I've bumped into her on many occasions since. Judging by the smile on her lips, I think I can guess.

Anyway, the next thing I knew I was coming round after surgery. My leg was in some pain and upon calling for help I was told that the operation was more serious than first believed. My knee was the size of Hattie Jacques. I asked for more painkillers; fortunately this time the oral form were administered.

In the end I required three operations on the knee. For a while they even considered replacing my kneecap with a plastic one; a move that would have ended my career. Eventually, however, I was able to begin my recuperation at Lilleshall Sports Rehab Centre; a place where many other sportsmen were coming to terms with similar setbacks.

I was lucky to have an excellent surgeon in Nigel Tubbs. I'm told he was the best available and I consider that he revived my career. He also oversaw my recuperation, often meeting me at 6.30 in the morning to chat and check on progress. He could tell me how I was feeling before I had said anything. From then on I would hit the gym at 8.30am, with experts to tell me just which exercises were suitable. They made my progress far more rapid. I had to wear an 18-inch knee support, complete with metal bars and hinges, whenever I bowled through the rest of my career, but it was a small price to pay. Before the operation I could hardly walk without experiencing sharp pain.

The other thing that was crucial was meeting top sportsmen in a similar position. We worked together in the gym, in the swimming pools or cycling, all supporting one another's attempts to get their lives back on track. It was a time of huge uncertainty for us all and some of them had experienced far worse than me. Ian Durrant, for example, in my opinion a man equal to England's Paul Gascoigne on the pitch, who played football for Rangers, had a dead man's Achilles tendon stitched on to his cruciate ligament to try and make it stronger. Durrant had scars resembling tramlines in his knee. The physiological problems in his case were a major part of his failure to resurrect his career for another three years. Quite a few of the guys never made it back into their sports at all and there were many times during the nine month period on the sidelines when I questioned whether I would be one of them.

There are so many ways a career can be ended in an instant. Perhaps the most bizarre incident that I know of involved the South African left-arm fast bowler Steven Jeffries. On his day Steve was unplayable, a wonderfully destructive bowler, and many supporters will remember his match-winning display in the Benson & Hedges Cup final of 1988 when his five for 13 helped Hampshire beat Derbyshire. I got to know him pretty well in Cape Town and was shocked when his pet Doberman dog bit off two fingers on his left hand, the ones needed to grip the ball. He never played again.

Having survived a slightly more prosaic injury scare, my attitude changed. I took advice from some of the sportsmen I'd met about how to survive the constant impact that life as a fast bowler demanded. I watched the likes of Graham Dilley - a bowler with the ability to bowl really fast - as he altered his approach somewhat to extend their careers.

I no longer tried to bowl fast every delivery. I mixed it up more. I served up a 'bag of lollies' to batsmen if I thought I could fool them into giving their wicket away with an extravagant shot.

I was no longer a player for the long haul. I decided I would be an 'impact player', that I would wait until I spotted the key moment and then give everything to win the vital passage of play. The bigger the occasion, the more I would rise to the challenge.

That wasn't the case at the start of my career. I threw myself into every single moment of every game with all the enthusiasm you would expect of a young man fulfilling his dream.

When I was fit, the professional game lived up to all my hopes and expectations. It was as exciting as I had ever hoped and I was soon making a contribution to the team that I loved. It wasn't long before I broke into the first team and was living the life I'd always wanted. It didn't disappoint.

One of my earliest one-day games was at Colchester against a strong Essex side that we very rarely beat in those days. I was only able to play as a batsman due to my back problems, but I was soon grateful for that as Essex blasted a record 299 for four from their 40 overs. Ken McEwan made an unbeaten 156 and some of our bowlers took a fearful mauling. At the end of their innings Essex's Ray East came into our dressing room with a paper cup. On it were Anton Ferreira's bowling figures in their innings. Eight overs for 85 runs. Ouch! A new - and most unwelcome - league record, and one that had previously been held by East.

It was a brave gesture from East. Ferreira was a powerfully built man, weighing in at 18 stone, and had boxed to a high level. He used to reminisce about his bout with the great Gerry Cotzee. Apparently Anton heard the bell, the pair touched gloves and he was promptly knocked out by the first punch. "I saw fuck all, man" he would say. Perhaps that's why he became a cricketer and not a boxer.

Anyway, a few hours after East's cheeky presentation we were laughing. I was at the crease as we passed their total; scoring 301. A monumental effort. I had always felt we could win and it was the first example of a side playing as a unit and overcoming a team that may have been - on paper - superior in terms of individual quality. It showed what could be achieved if we worked together.

Another humorous incident from that trip came when the public announcer told the crowd: "Warwickshire wicketkeeper Geoff Humpage has just let through his 50th bye in this Essex innings." Humpage was less than impressed, but it made the rest of us laugh.

Humpage was a great guy to play with. He helped me a lot, particularly in my early days, both with bat and ball. Humpty was excellent under pressure and his free spirit as a person meant that even the darkest situations were lightened. I remember one testimonial game where thousands of spectators turned up and people were spilling over the boundary rope. Suddenly the air was split by Humpage's ex. She gave him hell, tearing in to him in front of all the supporters and both sets of players. After a few minutes she turned on her heels and walked away. Anyone else would have felt cowed into silence, but not Humpage. He ran over to the groundman's shed, picked up an old fashioned broom - much like a witches' broom - and shouted after her: "Ingrid. Wait. You've forgotten your transport." We all fell about.

A particular highlight of those early days came during a match between us and Lancashire at Edgbaston when Muhammad Ali came to have lunch with us in the pavilion. The boxer was in the city to open a community centre named in his honour in Handsworth and thought it would be interesting to stop in and watch some cricket. At that time he was one of the most famous people on the planet and had amazing presence. I was only 21 at the time and have to say that the experience was pretty overwhelming. Like most sports people, I was in awe of this incredible athlete who had achieved so much in and out of the ring. Sitting down and eating right next to him remains one of my most cherished experiences. Parkinson's disease was already beginning to tighten its grip on him and he had a team of personal assistants to help cover up if he over-balanced or struggled with his movements. That famous wit was as sharp as ever, though, and I think I can speak for all of us in the room that day when I say it was a humbling experience to see how such a great athlete coped with the onset of the illness. The Lord giveth and the Lord taketh away. The greatness remained, however.

All these experiences were what my dad had helped me work towards. All those early mornings travelling to games or net sessions, all the chats about the game, all the kit he had provided and the time he had waited for me; all the investments seemed to have paid off as I lived the life of my dreams.

During the latter stages of my dad's life his health deteriorated drastically. Many problems stemmed from a failed triple heart by-pass. This operation may have prolonged his life by a few years but it was very much a case of quantity rather than quality. Many months were spent visiting him in hospital after complications set in. Leaving Edgbaston after a game on the day he had nine hours of heart surgery, I drove to the local Queen Elizabeth Hospital.

The scene wasn't pretty. My dad was heavily sedated, lying asleep as I sat next to him. When he came round and recognised me, his immediate response was to ask me to give him five minutes so we could slip out down the fire escape. He wanted to be at home with my mother. I laughed, not at the comment; more at the lengths my dad would go to make sure mom was ok.

I took him to so many hospital appointments. It became a mental battle. We both realised nothing could be done. A blood clot caused him agony; he would double up no matter where we were. Breathing was a major task, especially if he had to walk. I saw him in a state of breathlessness normally associated with people who had just run a marathon; it would happen to dad when he had to walk to my car.

On one hospital visit a specialist looked at dad's notes. After a quick examination he said that my dad's heart had failed, that there was very little time left. He left the room. It was a pretty cruel way of breaking the news.

Eventually dad was taken into hospital where he stayed until he passed away. Driving away from the hospital on the Sunday morning he died it seemed so surreal that despite what had happened, the world just kept on moving. People were laughing and going about their merry way.

The night before he died I rang the hospital; he always wanted to know the result of any game I was playing and how I had done. On this particular day I'd scored a big

MUHAMMAD ALI AT EDGBASTON

Ali, shown here with my skipper Bob Willis, made a surprise visit to Edgbaston. He walked through our door just before lunchtime one day. His was arguably the most famous face in the world - and the last we expected to see - never mind meet. I sat down next to the legend while we ate. Like virtually everyone else in the world, I had watched Ali`s life develop. It proved to be a very educational few hours.
I'll always be greatful to Bob. I was gutted when he retired; it felt like the lead singer had left the band. I reckon that had he remained at Edgbaston for another three years as a player my career would have benefited immeasurably and gone up another notch. Sadly he contracted Hepatitis in Pakistan over the winter of 1983-84. He had endless tests in clinics specialising in tropical diseases but the one thing that was apparent was a real lack of energy. After the season's final fixture we carried him in his chair from the changing rooms up to the ground's main bar where we sat and drank, celebrating his career and achievements.
He was an inspiration to me long before I arrived at Edgbaston. When I was a boy, Bob made a few visits to my family home to see my brother. At this stage Bob was someone who I'd only ever seen on television and I had listened with awe as my brother recounted various amazing deeds of England's quickest bowler. A decade-and-a-half later Willis said publicly on several occasions that I should be playing for England. It meant a lot.
By the time I signed for Warwickshire, Bob knew what worked best for him. He had struggled with nerves and fitness earlier in his career, often because his head had been filled with crap from other people. He knew the importance of encourage-ment. He, more often than not, showed his class when it really mattered. I was in awe of a guy I was now spending time with professionally and socially.
On my wedding day I shared a last bottle of wine with him; a way to thank him for all the things he'd done for me in the early part of my career as a professional

sportsmen, often tongue-in-cheek. That drink caused a first disagreement with my new mother-in-law. She thought I should have been somewhat more attentive to my new wife. I guess I had more in common with my ex-skipper.

I went along to support Bob at the club's Extraordinary General Meeting at the National Exhibition Centre when 'rebels' were trying to overthrow the committee. He delivered a strong speech, pulverising the club's management and committees. I recall someone saying to me that it proved that he didn't care about the club; to me it proved the very opposite. He cared so much he was prepared to put himself on the line and take a risk. In the end he lost the vote and his involvement with the club declined. Damn shame. There were too many senior individuals covering their own backs at this time. They made sure their own places were safe, be it in the team, as part of the coaching staff or on a committee. They were dark days in the club's history. And because Bob didn't win, the remnants of those problems linger to the present day. There were so many times when Bob returned to play for Warwickshire exhausted. He was never the most athletic fast bowler, so he had to work hard to produce the pace for which he was known. His lengthy run-up and somewhat ungainly action took it out of him and our own supporters used to criticise Bob for not trying. That's bollocks; he was often mentally and physically drained. He was an advocate of central contracts long before they were even on the agenda and would certainly have benefited from them. He played at a time when the game could often, very often in fact, be more of a grind than any kind of spectacle. I knew that I'd miss his presence when he retired. I was right.

hundred and also taken wickets. At six o'clock the next morning he died. I never scored another century. Dad was cremated soon afterwards along with various England and Warwickshire caps I'd acquired over the years.

Much later, when I looked through dad's old diaries it reminded me of an argument I'd had with him when I said I wanted to try and work as a roadie for American rock band Van Halen instead of going to Warwickshire. He'd gone nuts and history says he won that argument. Since he'd introduced me to the game as a kid I'd scored over 35,000 runs and taken over 2,000 wickets. Every game I'd ever played he'd recorded either in a diary or notebook, no matter how big or small. I obviously had a lot to thank him for.

At the start of my career, pre-season training consisted of a morning in a crowded three-lane indoor practice facility; the area was incapable of housing the 33 members of the playing staff. Surfaces would have no 'give' and often our bowling attack sustained injuries which would rule them out of games once the season commenced. Fitness training consisted of running 20 times around the local university's running track. Often it was freezing; regularly it was pouring with rain. Those of us under 19 years of age also had to run back from the university. Sometimes older players would leave after they had batted in practice. The explanation I heard was that there was some tidying up to do from their winter jobs.

Some days I felt professional sport wasn't glamorous at all. It was years before terms like "warm downs" or "ice baths" were common around cricket grounds. Instead it was part of our schedule to drink beer in a local pub in the afternoons to bond and increase team spirit.

Despite all this, I had a great time. I learnt a lot and was given a privileged education by my first Edgbaston captain, Bob Willis, and team manager, David Brown. I was rated by this pair; I wanted to learn from them. It's maybe why I asked them so many questions.

Later in my career, pre-season training consisted of flights to exotic places. We enjoyed outdoor, warm-weather practice without fear of injury and played high-quality games against decent opposition. We spent much time in South Africa but also went to Zimbabwe, the Caribbean and Spain. The only similarity with the 'good old days' was that we drank beer together.

During one of my earliest games within professional cricket I witnessed how dressing rooms can be far more than just a place to change, shower and talk tactics. The second XI changing room at Edgbaston was a hive of activity, with pranks being played on a daily basis. The side had a young fast bowler by the name of Keith McGuire, a local lad, tall and thin with a ferocious stutter which appeared at its worst when under pressure.

Keith had a damaging habit of over-stepping the crease and bowling no balls. To combat this particular inconsistency, the team coach cut a piece of string to the perfect length of his run-up. Over the next month our young fast bowler fastidiously marked out his approach to the wicket before the start of each game by using the string and some white paint. His no-ball problems disappeared and a more confident performer started to appear; one who looked to have a career ahead of him. Until, that is, a prankster within the ranks decided to play a trick.

At the start of our next home fixture our captain led his team out onto the famous Edgbaston turf. Fielders took to their usual positions, awaiting the familiar sound of the umpire shouting "Play" and the game to commence. Keith ran in to deliver. "No Ball," shouted the official. This was Keith's first for some time, in fact the first since he started using his inch-perfect piece of string.

Next delivery Keith also over-stepped. And the next... and the next. Some bastard within the side had cut a few inches off his string. Unfortunately the guilty party failed to keep hold of the bit snipped off and Keith's career came to an end soon afterwards. My one memory of this particular match is Keith standing, looking at where his feet were over-stepping, shouting "Fuck". The moment seemed funnier because his stammer made the word take three times as long to come out. The cruelty of professional sport. Keith was working a till in Lloyds bank within 12 months.

The mighty West Indies side toured England that summer. I watched from the back of the indoor school at Edgbaston as Colin Croft bowled to fellow Guyanese Faoud Bacchus. I stood with Derief Taylor, father of Lord John Taylor, later a senior politician in nearby Solihull. As each delivery Croft propelled nearly decapitated Bacchus, who was bravely batting without head protection, the bowler would stare without emotion and Taylor repeated the word "mean" in his deep Jamaican drawl. It was a perfect description of Croft. The batsmen's reactions were like fork lightening, pure self-preservation. I remember hoping that I never saw such bowling. I never played against Croft, but as my career panned out I played against plenty as good, as fast - and as hell bent on truncation.

They used to say that Croft would kill to get wickets. He came close on a few occasions. During a Test Match in Christchurch against New Zealand, after an appeal for a nailed on caught behind was turned down, he'd deliberately barged into umpire Fred Goodall. If the same happened nowadays the culprit would probably kiss goodbye to the rest of their career, but at that time the fast bowlers - be they from the West Indies, Australia, South Africa or

Nottinghamshire - seemed wild and frightening. Learning to bat against them was desperately difficult, a test of mental strength and bravery as much as talent and technique.

Early on in my career I recall batting in a tight run chase against Somerset, whose team included the giant 6' 8" West Indian fast bowler Joel Garner. Whilst he was out of the bowling attack we took the opportunity to smash their bowlers to all parts. One bowler, Colin Dredge, went for 49 runs in only 24 deliveries. When Somerset's captain Brian Rose brought back Garner, I decided to charge down the wicket to attack. Within the blink of an eye my stumps were cartwheeling out of the ground. I didn't see the ball from the moment he let go of it.

I knew I could prosper at this level, though. During that first summer I played against Andy Roberts, an Antiguan with a reputation who was then representing Leicestershire. It was with slight trepidation that I sat waiting to bat. He was quick, clever and cunning. When the moment did come, he nearly cleaned me up on several occasions with balls targeting my head, bowled with searing pace and accuracy. Somehow I made 59, however, to become the second youngest player ever to score a half-century for Warwickshire. To prove it was no fluke I made the same score in the second innings. I belonged in the game and at the club. I was happy.

It was also a delight to play with some of the characters around Edgbaston at the time. I recall a game at Scarborough in my early Warwickshire career when we were playing against a strong Yorkshire side. I watched as Alfy Sam opened our innings, smashed the first five balls to the boundary ropes, only to be dismissed off the next ball. The rest of the morning session carried on without alarm or entertainment except for a gale which froze anyone stood out in it. Finally the umpires called lunch. Both teams sat down to eat, only to see salad being offered. If ever there was a day you wanted hot food it was that one. I heard Alfy tell the waitress, "Sam don't eat bush." She replied, "You'll eat what you are fucking given, love." My team-mate Sam left the table cussing in Jamaican slang, something about a "bumba clart". The room fell about laughing. In fact laughter was something I always associate with Sam. Every time I looked at him on the pitch I'd laugh; his oversized team cap perched on his fine afro.

I was by now infatuated with a sport that was ingrained in me. I'd left my hometown, an area obsessed by sport, eager for success and adventure. And I was lapping up every moment, every taste, every lesson and every experience that life was showing me. They were uncomplicated times; the smile on my face as broad and genuine as any fun loving 20 year-old's on the planet.

Wasted?

Wasted?

PEOPLE TELL ME I wasted my talent. I've lost count of the times people have said that to me. Always men. Often barely functional, feral types whose own careers hardly bear scrutiny. I won seven trophies. There are few, very few, sportsmen who can match that. Of those that can boast that level of success, a fair few played in the same side as me.

Being described as an under-achiever had a massive effect on me. It still clouds opinions now. I heard it so many times that occasionally the emotions thrown up by criticism would be with me when I walked out to bat or ran in to bowl.

One thing I have learned: if you are trying to coax the best out of someone the worst thing you can do is under-mine them by telling them they're an under-achiever. I never do that in the sessions I run now. It's damaging, counter-productive and the person doing the criticizing should be looking at their own performance.

It's also a facile criticism. I've even read that the likes of David Gower and Ian Botham have under-achieved! Usually the comments are made by journalists who drink beer for half the day and have no idea how hard it is to per-form on the pitch.

It's no coincidence that the period at Edgbaston when we had the most success was when we had the most encouragement. I recall playing one of my early second XI games for the club. The game lost, we sat in the dressing room as the coach, Neil Abberley, tore into us in turn. "You're shit," he said slowly pointing to one player. "You're shit," he said to the next. Eventually he went round all 11 of us handing out his words of wisdom. Job done, he then left the room. Alan Oakman, who was the club's senior

BATTING AGAINST SOMERSET

Sometimes the unorthodox gets the best results. This picture was taken at Edgbaston in a season I scored over 1,000 runs. I've struck the ball so hard that the momentum has taken me off my feet. The bowler is Stephen Booth, a guy who was on the Lord's groundstaff at the same time as me. The Yorkshireman was also my drinking partner at the Three Horse Shoes public house in Hampstead. A great guy, a talented bowler and a good mate who could have had a longer career if maybe given better handling and advice. This doesn't look as if it was one of his better deliveries, though. Wicketkeeper Trevor Gard, a lovely down to earth guy who suddenly found himself in a team with superstars like Ian Botham, Viv Richards and Joel Garner, is standing on the next cut strip.

coach at the time, lightened the atmosphere when he broke the silence. "I suppose he thinks I'm shit, too," he said, typically trying to take the heat off us youngsters. But none of us ever forgot what was said by Abberley that day or the appallingly destructive environment such uncon-structive comments can engender in a dressing room.

They were unhappy days for the club. In fact the whole of the 1980s weren't great. From 1981 to 1983 Warwickshire went 35 Championship matches without a win! We went three years and nine months without a single win in a Championship game at Edgbaston. Even then our form hardly improved. Between 1986 and 1988 we went 24 first-class games away from home without winning. It's perhaps not surprising that our supporters were fed up.

We were bottom of the Championship table in 1981 and 1982. Although 1983 saw us jump many places to end the season in fifth position, it was clear that one-day cricket was to be our only realistic chance of competing and win-ning. We made it to the final of the NatWest Trophy in 1982, not least thanks to a brilliant century from my brother David in the semi-final victory over Yorkshire - perhaps the most public demonstration of his talent - but I was left out of the XI in the final because I was deemed to be "too young". I was 18 at the time. We did enjoy a decent run in the 1984 Benson & Hedges Cup too and, though we were well beaten by Lancashire in the final, it did at least give our supporters something to cheer.

During the semi-final at Headingley in 1984 I took a diving catch inches off the floor off the bowling of Bob Willis to dismiss their dangerman David Bairstow. He had smashed it as hard as you'll see; luckily my young eyes picked the ball out of a backdrop of thousands of coloured t-shirts and I was able to dive forward and the ball stuck in my right palm. It turned the game. We knew it; the Yorkshire team knew it and, unfortunately for me, so did thousands of their supporters stood only a few feet behind me. After our team celebrations and a few words of wisdom from Willis we returned to our fielding positions. Soon afterwards I chased a ball flat out along the boundary rope when suddenly a full can of beer flew past my face; it stopped me in my tracks. Bewildered, I watched as the ball trickled over the rope. Willis was in the distance shouting "stop the fucking ball, stop the fucking ball!" He hadn't seen the can.

Running off with the match won a few minutes later, several Yorkshire supporters tried to hit me and wrestle me to the ground. "Fucking southerner," snarled a voice. "I'm from Newcastle," I replied. "A damn lot further north than you." "You don't look like it," they said. What they meant I've no idea.

Back in the changing room the physio was examining Willis. Despite the fact that our captain had been bowling minutes earlier, his body felt icy cold. He clearly wasn't well after contracting hepatitis in Pakistan the previous winter. It was the illness that ultimately led to his career ending; the final at Lord's was his last game for the club. Despite that, some of our supporters felt that he simply wasn't trying. Nothing could be further form the truth. Other people would have been in hospital.

That game at Lord's - my first appearance in a final at the home of cricket - showed an example of the lack of communication at this time. I had been batting in the middle-order in that competition but, with 20 minutes to go until the start of the game, I was told I was opening the batting. I was completely unprepared. I was in the MCC offices cashing a cheque at the time and was told, "Smithy, you're opening the batting mate, pad up quickly". Hardly ideal. Later I bowled what, thus far, was the quickest spell of my career. It was motivated by pure anger that such a special day had been ruined by a rubbish pitch and some dodgy indecisive decision-making. To sum things up - John Abrahams, the Lancashire skipper, was awarded the Man Of The Match award despite being dismissed by me for no score. He didn't bowl either. The day felt like I'd been involved in a Monty Python sketch lasting many hours.

Anyway, despite occasional cup runs, supporters grew increasingly disenchanted. By the end of the 1987 the disgruntled members called a special meeting to debate a vote of no confidence in the committee and the chairman. The meeting, which took place at the Metropole Hotel at the National Exhibition Centre just outside Birmingham, was in part a reaction to the form of the team. But it was also a reaction to the club's inability to recruit the best players on the market - the failure to lure Botham to Edgbaston was certainly a catalyst - and the manner of the appointment of David Heath as secretary of the club. In the end the committee survived - they won the vote by 507 to 450 - thanks largely to an impressive speech from the club's chairman, Bob Evans. Ironically, it wasn't long before the committee got rid of Evans, too. When he decided they would all have to declare their interests in the club they voted him out of office while he was away on holiday.

At that special meeting, a supporter challenged MJK Smith, a former Warwickshire and England captain and chairman of the cricket committee. "Why has Paul Smith been shunted down the team's batting order just a few games after becoming the youngest ever to score 1,500 runs?" the supporters asked. Good question, I thought to myself. But MJK explained that I was no good at playing the short ball. He said I had been hit twice the previous season. What he didn't say was that I was on my way to nearly 2,000 runs and that I, like most batsmen, would gladly have swapped 1,000 runs per blow. Besides, with some of the fast bowlers plying their trade in county cricket at the time, it wasn't bad to get off that lightly.

I couldn't believe that MJK - who later became chairman of the club - was showing so little support to me in such a high-profile public meeting. A supporter came up and said to me, "MJK`s just slaughtered you in front of all these fans." It was humiliating. Smith was, basically, saying I wasn't good enough to open the batting. That despite the fact that I'd set records in the position the previous season; it was quite a slap in the face. I thought I'd brought a lot to the table as an opener. Coming out to bat without fear when your side is in front is one thing, but going out to bat without fear and playing shots when there are no runs on the board is quite another. My record deserved more than

Wasted?

BOB WOOLMER WITH (from left)
SHAUN POLLOCK, BRUCE McMILLAN AND ALLAN DONALD

We were all coached by Woolmer - and no-one loved the sport like Woolly. His mentor during his own playing career had been Sir Colin Cowdrey. Apparently Cowdrey used to tell the young Bob that, in order to progress; we should "make this season's weaknesses next summer's strengths." That's a great way of thinking and one which obviously worked for Bob, who started his career as a number 10 or 11 for Kent and later scored Test centuries batting at three for England.

When Bob became coach at Edgbaston he taught us bowlers how you need to keep your nerve and remember game plans, whilst being flexible enough to adjust to last-second innovations by batsmen. Bowling at danger stages of a game will see ups and downs, but in time the good days far outweighed the bad for us.

What Woolly exposed in us were our personal strengths and weaknesses. Sometimes I think we shocked him with what he might have perceived as a lack of professionalism. During a team meeting at Headingley, Bob asked each of us how many units of alcohol we drank a week. Our answers surprised him - maybe it was our honesty. Clearly he thought we drank too much. We had always been a social bunch, however, and our fitness helped our recovery time. A friend who spent quite a bit of time with me during my benefit year said he reckoned I had drunk about 120 pints the previous week, certainly in excess of 100. And, he warned me, I was on track to drink more in that current week.

Bob used to say that the breakfast of champions is muesli. I couldn't agree with that. I'd been brought up to believe that competition was the breakfast of champions. Soon afterwards I answered a questionnaire for that year's 'Cricketers' Who's Who'. I said I did not believe eating bowls of muesli would make me a better cricketer. It caused much laughter in our changing rooms when it made print. It was partially why I wrote it as things like diet were never far from Bob's thinking. In jest I'd often tell Woolly in front of the changing room that the brain uses more energy when you sleep than in waking hours. It's true.

a cheap slur on such an important evening for the club and had the effect of disincentivising a guy that was, at the time, as eager and enthusiastic a player as the team could have wanted.

Edgbaston was a place stuck in the past. The players' changing rooms were still segregated until the end of 1987. Until then county capped and uncapped players changed in different rooms, creating a division within the squad. The younger players had to knock on the door of the other dressing room if they wanted to go in! It was an unhealthy environment.

After new coach Bob Woolmer arrived things were different. He made a point of encouraging us and generating a positive atmosphere in the dressing room. That really is half the job of a coach. Once the spirit is right, it's also much easier to suggest technical or tactical changes.

I suppose deciding on whether I under-achieved depends on how you define success. If success is earning money, then I made - and lost - a fortune. A colossal fortune if you priced up the lifestyle. However, check out how many sportsmen don't win anything in terms of silverware throughout their careers; the pile stacks as high as the Eiffel Tower. A training ground car park full of Lamborghinis and Ferraris will often hide career under-achievement, smugness and mediocrity. Just because someone wears the Gucci name doesn't mean they have class.

I have been told that I am selfish a few times, too. Maybe. But I wasn't a selfish cricketer. Had I been I might not have been seen to 'waste' my talent. I could have played for my average, in doing so I might have excited a few cricket statisticians. I might even have impressed a few selectors. I'm not really one for bean counting. I just wasn't built that way.

So often the emphasis is wrong in sport. In team games like football and cricket, the team should be everything, but so often the focus is on individual achievement. You see it all the time, a batsmen grinds out a century, but it doesn't help the team win. Think about all those record-breaking innings, Lara's 375 or 501 for example. His team

BATTING, AGED 22

I'm about 22 here. I'd already broken several records, but I also already felt that I was lacking support in my career and life. I wasn't in control of my own destiny. I knew at this stage I'd have a career with peaks and troughs. This particular summer I'd become the youngest ever player to score 1,500 championship runs and I could also bowl a ball damn quick. Andy Moles and I set a number of records with opening partnerships, yet encouragement came only in terms of another year's playing contract. Within months I'd been moved down the order to accommodate others; the second time in two years I was demoted after success as an opener. From then on I just blanked out all the comments I heard about unfulfilled talent. Later in my professional career when we were challenging for all competitions I didn't envy our openers the job because of the amount of intense play we were involved in. By then I'd have been unable to perform that role well enough due to additional bowling pressures all-round players endure.

didn't win either game. Lara, however, in my experience, is someone I'd always want in my team. He is generally a match winner of the very highest order. In fact, Lara's been a match winner from the time he first picked up a bat.

I remember my former playing colleague Denis Amiss`s final season of first-class cricket when I was still a spring chicken as a sportsmen in the Warwickshire first team. Everywhere we played the talk was about how many runs he required to set a new record for a batsman - or even just a Warwickshire batsman - at a certain ground. It took all focus away from why we, as a team, were there, though I should stress that it was hardly his fault. But there's no doubt that it was a distraction from what was ultimately important. It had become about one man. It shouldn't be a surprise that we won fuck all for years with that sort of attitude prevailing. One guy even carried a banner bearing the statement: "Amiss-shire".

Statistics are fine, but they can't tell you if a player won games under pressure. My own career stats across all forms of cricket prove the point; a batting average of 25.16 and bowling average of 32.49. Nothing special when held against the greats of the game, but what do stats tell you? They don't say if my 12,603 runs and 517 wickets counted for anything; or more importantly, that they made me a match-winner; an impact player. I never allowed myself to forget that I was paid to entertain, either. Sometimes during my career I felt that but for a few colleagues, I may have turned up to play at the wrong venue, or that others involved were playing a totally different game.

Danny Blanchflower, Spurs' double-winning captain of 1961, put it best: "The great fallacy of the game is that it's first and last about winning. It's nothing of the kind. The game is about glory. It's about doing things in style, with a flourish, about going out and beating the other lot, not waiting for them to die of boredom." Blanchflower may have been talking about football, but the sentiment is equally valid in cricket.

I played with and against my heroes too and few can say that. In fact, I had a fair bit of success against the very same people I had watched on television as a kid. Those were the contests that most inspired me.

Does it concern me that I didn't play for England? Sure it does. Does it eat me up in the middle of the night? Hell, no. There's plenty more to life than that. I went where I was asked to play. In between I lived what some called "a fascinating existence". In recent times, a few young players - quite well known players - have asked me for "a master-class" in talking to women and making the most of every day and night. Such is my reputation, although it some-times feels as though it belongs to a different person; all those experiences are a lifetime away.

Some bog-average all-rounders have represented their country over the years. 'Bits and pieces' players; ones who wouldn't know how to grab a game by the throat if they tried, neither capable of impact or making their opposition hot under the collar.

Claiming I failed to utilise my talent is open to debate. I don't think people necessarily understand what my skill was. Sensing the moment in a team game was my strength, not plodding, or churning out statistics. Look at the trophies won.

Besides I did represent my country. Whether it was at age group level or in the Singapore or Hong Kong Sixes, I played in a fair few such games. If I started my career now I'd possibly have a central contract. The ability to bowl very fast whilst also being capable of scoring hundreds is pre-cious and would, I'm sure, have been appreciated by the more modern thinking England coaches of today. As it is, I was flogged to death in unforgiving sports halls and on featherbed English county wickets. After a run of 27 days cricket in a row, both first and second team, Gladstone Small and I were called in to see one of our coaches, Neal Abberley, who bollocked us for not trying! We were exhausted, but he either wouldn't or couldn't care. Not only did he want us to play every day, he wanted us to look as if we were enjoying it more. "Smile like you mean it" came to mind. In retrospect it's hardly surprising that I suffered career-threatening stress fractures to my lower back.

"SMILE LIKE YOU MEAN IT"

A phrase I heard over and over again from teachers as a kid at Junior School. It took me over two decades to understand what the teacher meant. I distinctly remember being dragged through the gates - away from my mother's arms - on my first day of school with the teacher saying "this is a battle we must win, Mrs Smith". I've had strong feelings about how to deal with kids ever since.

COACHING IN ARGENTINA

Here I'm demonstrating body position and movement in delivery. I always thought it was important to bowl shirtless when coaching youngsters, so they could see clearly how I positioned myself when I bowled. Some people have thought this was about vanity! It's another example of people criticising what they don't understand.

The profits of Bic pens and razors bought, amongst other things, these surroundings on a magnificent family estate on the outskirts of Buenos Aires as the company sponsored our sessions. Every Saturday we'd entertain hundreds of kids with cricket - they loved playing. They couldn't believe how fast I'd bowl a ball and would cheer if I knocked the stumps out the ground when I demonstrated to them. One old man who watched the work we did with Argentinean kids over a four-month period later contacted a British tabloid journalist to 'reveal' that I'd often sat listening to a walkman and coached in shorts during Bic sessions!

He forgot to mention that the numbers increased every time we put on sessions and that I was the only coach in the whole of Argentina. Now there are more than 100 cricket coaches working in South America.

GLADSTONE CLEOTHAS SMALL

A guy who cared about his cricket. The day we met we sat in the beer garden of the Plough in Harborne, Birmingham. Glad said nothing for three hours. He wore a miserable face having been "seen off" earlier in the day whilst batting to save a game during yet another Warwickshire defeat. When Gladstone lived at home with his mom. I'd often drop in for rice, pork and peas. On arrival his mom would shout upstairs: "Gladys, the owl is here," a reference to her belief I only came to life at night. The Bajan and I lived together for a couple of years, but it was when we went to Melbourne for six months he met his future wife, Lois. Their meeting transformed Glad. He gained confidence, stability and companionship. Lois once said that Gladstone spent at least a third more of his life sleeping than most men. I can vouch for that. When our team was batting he'd lie on the bed in the physio`s room and sleep. A few years after we'd both retired I faced Gladstone in a charity game, when I walked to the crease, I heard him shouting instructions on field changes. I shouted back, asking him how he could possibly know where I hit the ball, he'd missed 99% of my batting career through his sleeping habits. A man of strong beliefs - he declined the offer of joining an English rebel squad to play in South Africa under apartheid, turning down enough money to buy outright his beautiful family home.

NEW YEAR'S EVE 1984

Oscar Wilde said he could "resist anything but temptation."
I know what he meant. This trip to Australia was a great
experience. If Sydney has seen bigger or longer celebrations a few in attendance that night would like to hear of it.
A decade later a mate spent a summer playing in
Melbourne. During one game, after he'd delivered a short
ball at an opponent, the batsmen took off his helmet and
shouted back down the wicket "Just because you're black
doesn't mean you're fast, mate." A harsh testing ground
to ply one's trade.

ST. AUGUSTINE'S - CAPE TOWN, SOUTH AFRICA

The picture below left was taken at the time the South African Government was forced to dismantle Apartheid. Since I first spent time there ten years earlier, a mass of positives had arisen for people of colour. The playing field behind me was unused throughout the whole of this summer - we were forced to play all our fixtures on others' grounds. In the very same place now stands a community complex which is used as St. Augustine's' HQ. Over the summer I played with them, the feasibility of such a stadium was discussed a number of times in our changing rooms. A few team-mates from this time who worked within South African Government took these discussions further. Thankfully it worked. Nowadays two of the most notorious gangs in the Cape are kept separate by the complex's location and kids from these areas play safely within its perimeter walls.

NATWEST TROPHY WINNERS 1989

About 30 minutes before this picture was taken I'd shared a pint of champagne in a hospitality box with former England soccer legend Billy Wright. It had been a tense finish. With a hand-full of deliveries left, I said to Allan Donald that Neil Smith needed to smack the next ball out of the ground. Al and I watched as Neil duly did exactly that, hitting Simon Hughes for a huge six over mid off.
Within a few seconds we had won. At last! After being involved in two previous Lord's cup finals - one as 12th man - I finally had a winners' medal.

I WAS A FATHER WHILST A KID MYSELF

I've seen a million examples since I started working with young people or young adults. The first nights that this new-born boy spent at home were all sleepless, not because Oli was noisy; I just heard every rustle of sheets from his crib, every breath that he took. Over the following years I watched as he grew in character and spirit, this little chap came everywhere with me when I was around. Here we are with the three trophies Warwickshire won in 1994. Sport commitments took me away from my children during those precious years. It's time you can't claw back.

MOM AND DAD

My parents at their home in Selly Oak, Birmingham, with the Benson and Hedges Trophy. August 1994.
No father ever threw more balls at or offered more encouragement to a young cricketer. I had several coaches and all were good, but, other than Bob Woolmer, nobody made a greater impression on my career than my dad.
Winning at Lord's meant I'd finally delivered and brought home the Man of the Match award I'd promised my dad early in life.

CELEBRATING BRIAN LARA'S 501

Lara's draw-power and brilliance was breathtaking. He proved to be a champion of his sport and did much good work when with us - his unwillingness to be on call 24/7 made him unpopular with certain journalists, some of whom formed opinions without ever being within 80 yards of the man. It upsets me when I hear people suggesting that Lara wasn't a good team man - there's many who say things for personal gain or jealousy. He was excellent. There were so many occasions that he took the time to talk to team-mates to coax the best out of them. A few words from Lara's mouth often made a difference; 99% of the time it was uplifting. Yes, there a few problems between him and Derm, and yes, there were times that he was late. But the pressure on the guy was massive. He needed to be judged by different criteria. People should remember that he was the key ingredient in the club enjoying the most successful period in its entire history. So why the criticism?

DERMOT REEVE

No-one led men better than the guy from Hong Kong.
Dermot Reeve (left) was streets ahead of the pack.
Everyone who played at Edgbaston would want him in their
side - opponents tried everything to get to him - he loved
antagonising them!
We shared many experiences over our careers. Similar in
our wants - I thought he'd been more discreet than me at
one time, sadly that proved to be wrong. Dermot's on the
road to recovery from his drug problems now, which is
great as he has a lot to offer in a variety of ways;
as stimulator, activator, and a man who's brought results.

'TEXAS' TOM MOODY

Seen here at Lord's during the first of two finals we played against Worcestershire over that summer, the B&H final. Moody has narrowly avoided being run out from a deflection off my out-stretched hand. Tom and I had been team-mates earlier in our careers when the Australian spent a summer playing for Warwickshire.

During that summer the pair of us were rested for a game against Sri Lanka. Instead we commentated live on a show called Cricket Call with host broadcaster, Neil Manthorpe, on which fans could phone up to hear commentary. We struggled.

None of the three of us could pronounce the Sri Lankan names which took in anything up to 15 letters. At one stage there was a two minute period where we produced nothing but laughter. Each time we thought we'd regained our composure one of us would set the others off again. Anyone calling in for an update on play at Edgbaston must have thought they'd got through to the laughing hyena show. It's ironic really, a decade or so later, Tom was coach of Sri Lanka and is doing a brilliant job. Another Warwickshire team-mate Trevor Penny works as his number two.

OFFICIAL SOUVENIR BROCHURE

ANOTHER LORD'S FINAL

Trapping Graeme Hick lbw in the final of the Benson and Hedges Cup, Lord's 1994. I was Man of the Match in this game after taking three for 34 and scoring an unbeaten 42. Dermot was at the other end when victory was secured. A very happy day. Playing in a cup final at Lord's has the same meaning for a young cricketer as playing in the FA Cup final at Wembley for any soccer-mad kid. Lord's never once lost its magic and it's almost impossible to articulate the experience of playing there. The 31 year-old that walked out for his last final in 1995 felt all the same appre-hension and adrenalin of the nervous 20 year-old kid with wobbly legs and a dry mouth. The only difference 11 years later was that I had a wealth of experience behind me. This picture captures some of the emotion I felt knowing that I had just taken the crucial wicket. Hick was one of two men - Australian Tom Moody being the other - who single-handedly could have taken the game away from us. Note the clenched fists, and the almost skewer-like follow through, indicating the tension, importance and vitality of the moment. You'll see strikers do it after key goals.

EVER BEEN POOR?

It's rubbish. Trust me, I know. And I don't mean skint for a few days before pay-day. I mean no home, no food, nothing. I often went days without eating. After about 24 hours it doesn't hurt. In fact it hurts when you do have a meal. It proved a fascinating experience. This period confirmed to me that life is not a lucky dip; that things don't always work out alright. That there will not necessarily be a happy ending. People treat you differently when you're homeless. You appreciate the simple things in life; like any kind roof over your head. Having stayed in some of the most desirable locations in the world quickly paled into irrelevance. At least I found a place where, every time I woke, there'd be a camp fire nearby and faces which showed no menace. The safety of numbers was also a comfort.

TED HAYES AND THE HOMIES & THE POPz

Ted Hayes (above) believes so deeply in how cricket espouses virtues such as teamwork, self-worth and anger management that he founded a cricket team, the Homies & The POPz (below) in the gangland area of Compton, L.A. to coax youths out of entering a life of crime.

THE KID WON'T GET THE BALL

This kid went to retrieve a ball in a practice game, but when seeing where it had come to rest he turned and walked back to us. Why? Well, I walked over to get it myself and soon realised. There was a guy with an M11 sitting in a bush. You don't see many sub-machine guns among the climbing frames and rose bushes of an English cricket ground, but in LA this sort of weapon is all too common.

PRINCE CHARLES

The heir attended a Prince's Trust day at Edgbaston. The Prince joined in and actually had a bat - against England and Warwickshire's Ashley Giles and with the likes of Sajid Mahmood and Vikram Solanki watching on. Camilla Parker-Bowles asked me how to tamper with a ball. Eventually I showed Charles how to bowl - he has a fair wrist action!

ROGER DALTREY
Whilst dining with the legendary Who lead singer in London I learned of his massive support for the Teenage Cancer Trust.

GEORGE BEST
George kindly agreed to speak at one of my benefit dinners at Lord's. Those who said he wouldn't turn up should have had more faith in him.

JIMMY PAGE
Aged 15, I attended the very last Led Zeppelin gig. I didn't think for a moment that I'd end up captaining the lead guitarist's cricket team.

MICHAEL HUTCHENCE
Sex on legs. A fascinating man; intelligent, articulate, high octane, daring and a magnet for the opposite sex.

MY BEAUTIFUL KIDS

(Above left) Out in the middle at Edgbaston with Mikey.

(Top right) A chance meeting with my daughter, Levi, with whom I am allowed no contact.

(Above right) My first born, Oliver, with cricketing legend Ian Botham in South Africa.

(Below) The last time all four of us were together

In the mid-1980s there weren't many sides that could match the pace of our bowling attack at Warwickshire. In Bob Willis, Gladstone Small and me, we had the speed to trouble the best and, as Ian Chappell stated, "If you've got firepower, hand it out, because when you haven't you'll get it from those that have." But because most of our senior players were batsmen, the surfaces were prepared to suit them; slow, low tracks that made for attritional cricket. Those batsmen - and those playing surfaces - didn't help us win many games, though they saved a few. The outlook was always defensive.

Even when we had the opportunity to use our pace on fast wickets, often we were prevented from doing so by our captain. I remember Amiss, who, of course, was an opening batsman, standing at slip shouting "don't!" if we bowled short deliveries at opposing fast bowlers. He was appalled that we might be doing something to wind up our opposition, which would mean they bowled short back at us - more specifically him.

In one of my very early games versus Sussex I gave Imran Khan a real peppering of short deliveries. I broke his finger with one delivery and really let him have it. Whilst all this happened you could hear the moans from the batsmen as they realised what would come back at us later. I knew we had to try something different if we were to win this game. To be fair, Imran, Pakistan's bowling spearhead, responded by later producing a ferocious spell of bowling where he took six wickets for six runs off only six overs. We won the game, though.

To be fair, I did also see the same tactic backfire spectacularly. Andy Lloyd, never one to resist a flutter, had been quoted before the Lord's final in 1982 giving odds against Surrey's Sylvester Clarke making inroads with the new ball. It was a red rag to a bull and I knew he'd regret opening his mouth. He didn't bat for long and Clarke bowled like the wind.

Everyone knows how fast Bob Willis could bowl, but sometimes they don't appreciate how quick Gladstone Small could be. I remember playing a game against Surrey when I noticed that the batsman, Graham Clinton, was standing two yards out of his crease to try to disrupt Gladstone's length. "He's taking the piss, Glad," I shouted. "He doesn't think you're quick." The Bajan paused to observe the scene and flicked his arm towards the bats-man. "Get back," Glad warned. "Make me," Clinton growled. A brave, but ultimately foolish, phrase.

We watched as Glad returned to his bowling mark, 25 yards behind the stumps at the non-striker's end. He stopped and threw his mark back an extra couple of yards and then ran in. Charging in at his opponent with height-ened intent, he bowled a horribly fast and well directed bouncer that smashed into the batsman - still standing far closer to the bowler than was necessary - before he had any time to react. Fragments of his helmet fell everywhere and Clinton was forced to retire hurt. Glad could bowl a damn quick ball.

Dennis Amiss was a brilliant batsmen, make no mistake. Anyone who make over 100 first-class centuries has to be a bit special. I recall thinking what a shame it was he didn't go into coaching because he could pass on such incisive technical wisdom. But the records show that little positive was happening at Edgbaston on the pitch during that era; we were a poor side which once went 35 championship games without a win. For a team that contained interna-tional players such as Willis, Alvin Kallicharan and Amiss, it represented a shocking level of under-achievement.

Later, Dermot Reeve came into the side as captain. Although he was another who was well aware of his average, seemingly doing anything to protect it, he was, in many ways, the complete opposite to Amiss. An inferior technical player he may have been, but his ability to wind up the opposition and make things happen on the field led us to unprecedented team success. Reeve is, by some distance, statistically-speaking, the most successful captain ever to lead Warwickshire. By the same criteria, Amiss is second worst.

In Amiss' day, however, we were an old team. Along with Kali, Norman Gifford and Chris Old, we were in danger of becoming a retirement home for cricketers. Opposing

1989 WARWICKSHIRE SQUAD

Only Gladstone Small, of those on the front row, experienced the success that was to start with winning the Nat West Trophy in 1993. There are a few dodgy haircuts in there, aren't there? And Roger Twose looks as if he has been auditioning for a part in a 1970s porn film. A laugh was never far away in this squad. In a way that made our inconsistencies all the more frustrating. But it also made the bad times more bearable. We spent this pre-season training in La Manga, returning fit, buoyant and well confident. When we landed at Stansted airport I met and had a ten minute conversation with tennis superstar Bjorn Borg - a fascinating guy, who for his own reasons just quit his stratospheric career aged 25.
The coach, Bob Cottam, claims I once overtook him at high speed at a set of traffic lights in Cardiff. I was in reverse at the time. I might have got away with it had I not been in a sponsored car with graphics plastered everywhere.

crowds certainly thought so. We took the field at certain grounds to the sound of the *Dad's Army* theme, sung by opposition supporters.

Some people, though very few players, feel that one-day cricket is an inferior version of the sport. It's a myth, just look at the crowds attracted to such games around the world. Fast runs and wickets will turn and win these games. I've seen plenty of international players lose their bottle in situations thrown up by one-day cricket. The pressure is different, but often the standard is just as high. People who judge performers and their impact over a career should overview the players' impact on games, when it happened and, more importantly, if it brought home trophies.

At different stages of my career I was told I was close to being picked for England. Between 1989 and 1991 especially. Bob Willis, who captained me in my early career, said at the time of selection for the 1994-95 Ashes tour down under that he would have picked me ahead of Chris Lewis or Craig White. Wise man, Bob. He, along with a few other shrewd judges, had also previously described me as the "fastest white man" in cricket.

I must confess, however, that there were times when I felt I might have been gullible to believe the importance of the team ethic. Sometimes I felt like one of those poor sops who rushed down to the recruitment office to sign up for active service at the start of the Great War. They believed in the glory of "dulce et decorum est pro partria mori" but could have been forgiven for having second thoughts as they bled to death in some foreign field. Sometimes it seemed as if those who were selfless on the pitch just played into the hands of the more selfish, more worldly, members of our team.

Viv Richards once told me to think about myself a bit more. We were playing Somerset in a game at Taunton where he scored 322. After the Antiguan reached his century I asked him if he'd "had enough". "No," he replied - he was going to "stick around a little bit longer". True to his word, he did. He raced to his triple century off a further 140 deliveries. It was pure carnage. In reply I had put on over 160 with Amiss and was feeling good. But on 93 I was caught on the boundary trying to get on with the game. "Paul," Viv said with real feeling. "When you get that close, you've got to make it count."

My part in Warwickshire's success so very nearly didn't happen at all. I came very close to leaving the club in the early 1990s. When Dermot took over as captain there seemed to be quite a few all-rounders competing for few places and I knew that he, as captain, would always play ahead of me.

When I let it be known that I was thinking of moving, there was a huge amount of interest from other counties. I don't know how players in other sports first engage with potential new clubs. In my case a piece of paper from an opposing skipper was shoved in my hand. Some other club captains just rang me. Financial details were very much secondary; I simply wanted to play cricket to as high a level as possible and to win trophies.

I thought long and hard about going to two counties in particular. Worcestershire, just down the road and enjoying some success, was one of my options, while the other one was Durham. I was tempted to go, not least by the fact that Ian Botham would have been a team-mate. By this stage he had left Worcestershire and was one of a number of experienced players trying to raise the profile and standard of the side new to the rigours of English first-class cricket. Had I been single I would have joined them, though in retrospect I'm very pleased I stayed at Warwickshire. I would have missed all our successes just around the corner at Edgbaston.

In the end I was talked into staying at Edgbaston. I knew I was quite near a benefit, but that wasn't a major consideration because the money I would have earned elsewhere would have outweighed my Warwickshire salary. I didn't particularly believe what I was being told at Edgbaston, but I had a young family and moving would cause problems. Besides, I had always been a Warwickshire supporter and I knew the club would always remain close to my heart. Sentiment plays a greater part in such decisions than you might think.

A lot has been written and said about Ian Botham over the years. My own view, and the view of most of those who know him, is he's not the person sometimes reported upon negatively over the years, especially as a young man. Clearly he was a colossus as a cricketer, but it is as a compassionate man that he is most impressive. Recently he embarked on yet another long haul charity walk to raise many more millions for needy causes. He has helped save a great many lives. But there is so much more he does to help people privately that few people would ever know about.

Ian Botham's impact on me started as a 13 year-old kid when I'd watched him take five Australian wickets in a Test at Trent Bridge. The way he played the game made an immediate impression. All the talk amongst English cricketers at this time was of the young Somerset all-rounder, and he hadn't yet exploded into the performer he would soon become. Over the next few years his impact with bat and ball were sensational. One morning I was about to leave the house to do my morning paper round when my dad informed me of the all-rounder's performances in the Jubilee Test in India. The game had seen him take 13 wickets and score yet another hundred. Whatever Botham was made of needed to be bottled, studied, and analysed.

Four years later I watched from the players' dining room at Edgbaston as he took five for one against Australia to win a game that had appeared lost. Two years later I was playing against him.

I'd been promoted high up the batting order against Somerset in a B&H quarter-final at Edgbaston. The decision was a success and I scored a quick-fire 37 runs. Beefy bowled from the pavilion end early in this game, doing so with pace, aggression and skill. After I smashed him square of the wicket for a boundary, he bowled a much fuller delivery. I attempted to hit it back over his head, but only managed to drill the ball into my foot. It slowly rolled back down the pitch. Botham picked it up, looked at me and wrung his hand as if in pain. The crowd laughed; he was making fun of me!

When the game had finished I went for a beer with 'Beefy' and my skipper Willis. Warwickshire had won and I wanted to celebrate. I mentioned the incident on the pitch to Beef; he replied that if he could wind up Sunil Gavaskar on unresponsive surfaces in India, he was sure he could do the same to me. He told me to ignore it; it was part of the sport.

I first met Botham through Willis. As is often the case, I found that his public reputation was a long way removed from the real man. For a start, I understood that Beef loved a drink, but I never saw much justification for that rumour. He hardly drank at all and if alcohol was about it was drank in quiet rural pubs.

Only once did I witness his ability to drink in vast quantities. We were both in Cape Town one English winter and, after breakfast on top of Table Mountain, we moved to the Waterfront area. Five hours later I was out of the game, but he carried on into the early hours. On another occasion in Birmingham I recall him wrapping me in a blanket and putting me to bed in his hotel suite after I had drunk too much. This particular night had been spent with senior Durham players at a time when discussions were in the air about me returning north to play for them.

There was always a lot to talk about with Beefy. We both played attacking cricket and enjoyed life. It was a joint and obvious belief that it was important to persevere and look to impose, even intimidate, on the pitch. It was impossible to play with the spirit we both did, then turn into a different character after hours. We weren't chameleons. Over our careers we both did the business when it was needed, often when games were big. Fast runs and wickets rather than accumulating statistics. Botham may have played on bigger stages than me, but that wasn't my choice. Skippers threw our type the ball when they needed an immediate impact.

Botham had brought unprecedented success to Somerset. In partnership with Viv Richards and Joel Garner, he turned a club that knew very little about success into a dominant force in one-day cricket for several years.

In this era, Botham, Viv Richards and I were sitting in the sauna during heavy morning rain. It looked unlikely that we'd bowl a ball all day, when suddenly 'Taffy', our dressing room attendant, knocked on the door to inform us we were about to start. In the next hour or so I fielded as first Viv tore us apart with 50 in three overs, before Beef thrashed us for 138 off only 49 balls! If people have struck a ball harder and cleaner I've never witnessed it. It was murder.

It was one of the few times in my career I hoped the ball didn't come in my direction. Standing 80 yards from the bat, one ball came off Botham's bat at head height and I just moved out of the way. Any hand contact with that shot would have ended my season. The ball struck the seating and rebounded back past, nearly decapitating me on its way. In the end it rolled all the way back to the bowler. It was carnage of the highest order.

In the end it seemed as if the success of these three giants of the game was held against them at Somerset. These three superstars of their sport got treatment similar to that later handed out to Brian Lara during his time at Warwickshire. Whatever the causes, three of the best players the game has ever seen left the West Country club; it's hard to see how that helped the team.

Around this time we hoped Botham would sign for us, but in the end he went to Worcestershire. In many ways I thought he would come to Edgbaston, especially due to his friendship with Bob Willis and David Brown. Unfortunately I, and other young Warwickshire players, had to watch as his presence rubbed-off on his new team-mates as he helped bring many trophies to our local rivals at New Road.

My own career had started so well. At 18 years and 57 days, playing against Leicestershire, I became the second youngest man to make a first-class half-century for Warwickshire. At 19 years and 69 days I became the youngest man to make a first-class century for the club (a record broken, almost two decades later, by Ian Bell, who was 13 days younger) and at 20 I scored 1,000 first-class runs in the season. Then, as a 22 year-old opening batsman, I became the youngest man in the club's history to make more than 1,500 first-class runs in a season. Some of those records have since been broken; some haven't. Some, I believe, never will be.

Opening the batting with Andy Moles, we set records that had previously been held by such legends of cricket as Percy Holmes and Herbert Sutcliffe for the most consecutive opening partnerships in excess of 50. Yet, despite making such a success as an opening batsman, I was shunted down the order. The following season I even batted at seven! The reason? To accommodate the return of Andy Lloyd; another example of the needs of a senior player taking precedence regardless of the good of the team. It did for me as a first-class batsman. I was never the same again in the longer version of the game.

I'm not saying I would have been the best in the world. There were times when I realised just how tough a job batting against the best bowlers in the world was, but generally I felt the big occasion brought out the best in me. I remember going out for a drink with some of the Australian team one night and mentioning to Shane Warne that I reckon people are guessing most of the time when they face leg-spin. Their wicket-keeper, Ian Healy, piped up and said, "Don't worry, Smithy mate. Tomorrow I'll let you know what's coming each ball."

I thought nothing more about it until the next day when I walked out to bat with the team two wickets down. After a while Warne came on and the real challenge started. Healy, standing inches behind me, discreetly called each delivery as Warne let it go, so I was able to play with relative ease. Just a few balls in, however, Healy remained quiet and the ball thudded into my pads. Plumb lbw. I glanced up at the wicket-keeper and we immediately both burst out laughing.

As a bowler I took two first-class hat-tricks and on another occasion took nine for 56 in a day against Gloucestershire. The more memorable of the hat-tricks came at Eastbourne. It proved to be a great trip. Team-mate Neil Smith and I left the ground, visiting the nearby pier and buying everyone in the team a pair of espadrilles. It was to prove compulsory wearing for the duration of our stay.

During this trip I bumped into club chairman Bob Evans at about 6:30 one morning whilst walking on the beach. He, like me, was taking an early morning stroll, though it must have crossed his mind that I was just making my way back to the team hotel. He didn't mention it though; instead he greeted me with customary enthusiasm.

Later that day, on the final afternoon of play, I took my maiden first-class hat-trick. It occurred when the game appeared to be slipping away from us and with Sussex skipper Alan Wells at the crease on 144 not out. We had all played in games like this that drifted away and we needed someone to intervene. I was thrown the ball with the instructions: "As quick as you like, dear boy."

Within minutes of starting to bowl, my boot split. We were mid-way through an over but the umpire, Jack Bond, sighed: "Go and change the boot then." As I ran off I knew I didn't have a spare boot in which I could bowl fast. Returning to the changing room I sat down, smoked a Marlborough, drank a coke and scanned my footwear options. Should I wear a batting shoe and hope? Or should I borrow team-mate Tim Munton's size 12s? I opted for the Munton option and applied three pairs of socks; I wore size ten-and-a-half. After finishing a second Marlborough, I re-entered the arena.

By then quite a lot of time had passed without any action. I resumed by delivering a ball with such a lack of pace that it totally baffled Australian Tony Dodemaide and bowled him. It was unplanned; my foot actually slipped about three inches down the boot in my delivery stride. I'd over-balanced if the truth were known.

We had the breakthrough we needed. My next delivery was a fast, short ball which dismissed new batsmen Peter Moores. The hat-trick ball was again pitched short, the opposite of what the batsman expected, and was directed at the head of Tony Piggott. It was quick. And it worked.

First-class hat-tricks are a rarity. This moment of inspiration changed the course and result of the game. We soon acquired the 99 runs for victory, departing with a then maximum 24 points.

As the team relaxed in the changing rooms, I finished an interview with Radio One. Our chairman appeared and congratulated me on what had just happened, commenting, "Such performances are often achieved with far from ideal preparation." We both laughed.

My second first-class hat-trick came one hot morning. I was thrown the ball by my skipper Andy Lloyd. My instructions were to try to finish the game off as soon as possible. Within ten minutes we were off the pitch. I had taken four wickets in no time, including another hat-trick. There are only four people who've represented my team who have acquired two first-class hat-tricks. No mean achievement considering the Warwickshire club formed in 1882.

But perhaps the highlights of my playing career came at Lord's. In all I was involved in seven Lord's finals. We won four. Many players, even very good players, never have that privilege even once. I've been a lucky man.

In 1994 I found myself standing out in the middle with my skipper, Dermot Reeve. It was 14 years since I'd first set foot on the ground. I'd spent a season there on the groundstaff - as had Dermot - and knew the place well. I'll always be fond of it. The game was in the bag and within minutes we would be running off carrying souvenir stumps. Lord's was a place we both felt comfortable. On the day there were many people I knew in this special ground and soon I would have the chance to celebrate with them. I had taken three important wickets, bowled damn fast and turned the game in our favour. I'd followed that up with a brisk 44 runs.

Lots of things went through my mind; not least thoughts about my dad. I'd finally won the Man Of The Match award I had once promised him. He had done so much to get me to that position. Suddenly my thoughts were broken by an opponent. Australian Tom Moody, a former team-mate and good friend, walked past and said: "Congrats mate. It's in the bag; man of the match, enjoy it." Next ball we won. It was the first of three trophies we won that summer.

Receiving the man of the match award from adjudicator Sir Richard Hadlee meant a lot. It's maybe like Wayne Rooney receiving the equivalent trophy from Pelé. That's not to compare my level of ability with that of the brilliant Rooney, but that Hadlee was about as good an all-rounder as any in the business so it was especially rewarding that he should recognise the significance of my contribution. I felt Hadlee's decision vindicated my approach over the years. It proved that I performed on the bigger stage; when the pressure was on. Several international cricketers told me that there was more pressure on a player in a Lord's final than in a Test match.

My experiences there had not always been so happy. On my first visit I was left out purely because I was young and it was seen as being a reward for a senior player. On another occasion I gave some complimentary tickets to a friend only to see him rush on to the pitch and try to steal the stumps!

It is true that when fixtures lacked an atmosphere I struggled. It was a source of continued ammunition for my critics. Allan Donald, who was kind enough to say that I was the best all-rounder he played with, said publicly that he thought I found the game too easy and so struggled to concentrate. But surely it's not how long you spend in the office; it's what you do while you're there. AD and I would agree on that.

After the balcony formalities I was ushered into a press conference with Derm. It went on for ages; it was the first time Warwickshire had won the B&H. Frank Skinner and Dwight Yorke were among the team's supporters at the ground. Dwight had lost the keys of his hire car, though judging by the girl accompanying him, I don't suppose he lost much sleep over it. The car was a distant second in his list of priorities.

Many of us at Warwickshire had experienced much worse times. We had gone through seasons where we didn't challenge at all. Recent years had seen a massive turn-around in the quality of play and our success; we played bigger games, saw bigger crowds and won trophies. Everyone in the squad was confident and all our opposition were scared of us. I played the most effective cricket of my career in this era; I knew I could take wickets and score fast runs.

The first trophy in a spell of six in 25 months had landed at the end of the previous summer. We chased a record score, again at Lord's, and we'd got it. Our path through to that final had seen me play a significant part, the final was the same. Coming in at 18 for two I made a quick 60. Asif Din's century, quite rightly, took the plaudits, but I knew I'd played my part. Not that the fame did Asif much good. A little while later, at a cash point, he had a knife pulled on him. "Alright, Asif," the guy said before snatching his cash.

I was at the crease in 1995 when we beat Northants to win the NatWest final, too. There had been a difficult lead-up to the game and it had then spread over a second day, due to inclement weather. The whole team visited a restaurant in St. John's Wood, but my wife and I had left early, going in different directions after a row. The bad feeling lingered like a hangover all weekend. In retrospect it was probably not a good idea to alter our normal big-match preparations.

Anyway, having gone for a quick drink in Hampstead, I took a taxi back to the hotel and went to my room. There was a knock at the door and I let Keith Piper in. He was smoking a joint; I declined the offer to share. Not really the time or place. A little while later my wife came in and smelt the cannabis. She blamed me; a natural enough reaction, I suppose.

Sportsmen often aren't really prepared for real life. From an early age they are protected from the outside world, cossetted by clubs intent on giving them the best environment in which to perform at the top of their ability. Players hardly have to worry about their laundry, their car, their travel arrangements or accommodation. Most of the year, they even have their meals provided. All they have to concentrate on is their game. And that's probably just the way it should be.

The problems only occur when they finish playing. The vast majority won't make a huge amount of money from sport. They'll do pretty well for a few years but, in their early 30s, many suddenly find themselves out of a job and with no obviously marketable skills or qualifications.

The lucky ones might remain within their game. A few move into the media; some into coaching. But most have to start life again. It's not easy and we shouldn't be surprised that so many retired players run into potential trouble. David Frith has written a fascinating book, *By His Own Hand*, later re-published as *Silence Of The Heart: Cricket Suicides*, all about the cricketers who took their own life.

There were so many occasions in my own career when I've seen examples of fellow players behaving as if they had never previously stepped into the world outside a cricket ground. My old friend Gladstone Small was funny! I recall Gladstone buying his first car. He was ringing round trying to get it insured. Finally he tells me he's done it. How much, I ask. £1,200 says Gladstone, the same price as the car. You've overpaid, I tell him. Never mind, he says, it's done now and it's a one-off payment. He didn't realise that it was only for a year. We were young, naive yet so very experienced in other areas of life.

Another time `Glad` called me in an obvious state of panic. We were living in Melbourne at the time and he'd been driving down the freeway when suddenly he heard a huge bang from under the bonnet of his Land Cruiser. Did I have any ideas? I asked him how often he checks the engine oil. There was a long silence. You guessed it; he didn't know engines used oil!

He almost killed me one day. Driving from Eastbourne to Headingley for a big semi-final, Gladstone entered the Dartford Tunnel. Immediately, however, he became agitated that the radio has stopped working and starts meddling with the buttons. Peering down from the wheel to see what's gone wrong, he didn't notice the tunnel traffic had stopped; we ploughed into the back of the car in front. Straightaway someone goes into the back of us and before long we're involved in a huge pile-up which saw the whole tunnel shut for some time. When the mess was finally cleared, I asked Gladys if he knew why the radio had stopped working in the tunnel. He replied he didn't, adding, "They don't have tunnels in Barbados"!

He was a calming influence on me, however. Gladstone is such a laid-back man; I reckon he spends half his life asleep. There were times that even he would get wound up, though. He was the victim of a really terrible lbw decision at Edgbaston once and smashed his bat through the dressing room window on his return. What made it so funny though was that the bat became stuck and the more Gladstone tried to pull it out, the more stuck it got and the more angry he became. The rest of us struggled - without success - not to laugh at him.

Keith Piper wasn't much better than Gladstone. I remember a long car journey from Manchester during which he made a series of phone calls on his mobile. I remarked that it would cost him a fortune. He smiled. "No way," he said. "The phone's plugged into the car's cigarette lighter; it's a club car, the club will have to pay." Piper: great wicket-keeper, but not one of the sharpest minds of his generation.

I had loads of good times living with Gladstone. We shared a house for a few years. Us and a guy called Chris Lethbridge; 'Moon, Loon and Coon' they used to call us in those less politically correct times. I was Moon on account of being up all night. You can probably guess which one referred to Gladstone.

I guess we were fairly typical young bachelors. The house was a scene from the TV series *The Young Ones*; none of us were much inclined to spend an evening in doing the dusting. One month we had all refused to do any washing up; everyone waiting for the other guy to do his share first. The lack of dishes grew so bad that I recall heating up baked beans in a kettle on the stove. Later that night one of the guys brought a girl home for coffee and 'hors d`oeuvres'. He boiled the kettle, went to pour the drink only to see the remains of my meal floating on top of her hot coffee. It was seen as a personal victory in our childish avoidance of household chores.

Some people are reminded of periods in their life by a song; personally, I remember times from the cars I drove. I bought my first sports car when I lived with Gladstone. A red convertible MG. It hardly ever had the hood up. One rainy night I drove Gladstone to one of the local nightspots. He held an umbrella over us all the way to stop us getting wet. The faces on the queue of customers waiting to go in were a picture.

'Loon' was always making us laugh, though often not on purpose. After being left out of the 11 at Oxford he went to the local shops and came back with a collection of comics. Having removed his shirt to soak up the sun, he sat down for a gentle day of relaxation, but soon fell asleep. By the time he woke up he was horrendously sun burnt, but with a white patch on the middle of his chest where the comic had been.

He was sent home from a second XI game in Wales once. He had bought a water pistol and, after a fair few drinks, let loose during a team meal the night before the game. The coaches finally lost patience and demanded he travel home immediately. It took 'Loon' all night, five train changes and a hell of lot of explaining to the senior Warwickshire staff before he was forgiven. He also once complained that a pain-killing injection was "beginning to wear off". It had been administered three months previously.

He was a great guy. He could always make you laugh, no matter what the circumstances. He would probably be the first to admit he could have worked harder, though. During pre-season training Willis, trying to encourage him, bet 'Loon' £10 that he couldn't lose 10lbs in weight over the next week or so. Lethbridge raised a beer to the captain and said, "I bet you £10 I can't either."

I do feel I was lucky to play when I did. The game was less professional than it is now, but there had just started to be more opportunities for foreign travel and, with domestic cricket still on terrestrial television, we were probably more in the public eye than today's players. I just feel we had more fun than today's cricketers.

The life of a professional cricketer also allows you a lot of spare time. Some players struggled to make ends meet during the winter months and I know of two England bowlers who spent time working as a topless doorman and a gigolo. Another county player was an undertaker.

I spent one winter, after being advised I would have to rest my knee, working as a classic car restorer, opposite the workplace of Worcestershire's Martin Weston, who sold cars on a used car lot.

Cricket took me around the globe. South America, South Africa, Australia, the Caribbean and the U.S., to name a few places; it was all fascinating and taught me loads. Particular favorites were my times representing England in sixes tournaments. Hong Kong was a real experience. From the moment the plane seemed to be about to land in the middle of a busy street - anyone who ever flew into the old airport will know what I mean - to the moment I went home, I soaked up every moment of a wonderful, exciting city.

It was Tim Lamb who had phoned me to ask about my availability. I was immediately excited; the make-up of the squad sounded good, the timing of the event suited my schedule and being in Hong Kong was a bonus for the sights alone.

Within hours of arrival all the participating teams were taken out on a luxury boat trip around Hong Kong harbour. A superb banquet was laid on by the trophy sponsors and there was a great opportunity to mingle with both tournament and government officials in a relaxed atmosphere. One of those present was Chris Patten, the last Governor of Hong Kong. When I suggested to him that he might just have the best job in the world, he smiled.

That year's Hong Kong Sixes competition had been moved from Kowloon to the magnificent 40,000-seater Government Stadium in Hong Kong Central. The place was home to a colourful mix of nationalities, so the crowds supported all the teams pretty much equally. What was more, the games were broadcast on satellite television and the huge Asian audience added to the sense of importance for every player. Nobody wants to stuff up in front of that many millions.

During the first few hours of the tournament our side pulled off a couple of surprises. We wiped the floor with the West Indian and Australian teams - the two favorites for the tournament. I remember the burly New Zealand batsman Mark Greatbatch, later coach at Warwickshire, asking a guy to throw a ball at him so he could experience hitting it into the stands; he had only faced two balls in the series. And both had dismissed him.

Michael Hutchence had told me I'd love Hong Kong and he was quite right. The speed of the place was contagious and I thrived on the fact that it was a 24-hour culture. Michael actually had a place out there, and it wasn't hard to see the attraction.

One night all the teams went out for a drink together. Having spent some time in the bar with the dentist's chair made famous by Paul Gascoigne, we moved on. We were in quite a well known venue - Joe Banana's - but the place was so busy it was proving impossible to get service at the bar. One of the Australian players - later recognised as one of the finest batsmen in the world - jumped up on the bar, pulled his trousers down and shouted at the bar staff, "Do you see me now?" Funnily enough, it worked. He was served next.

I was also lucky enough to visit Bruce Lee's old house. It was already more than a decade since he had died, but his 1970s Rolls Royce remained on the forecourt.

At various times during the Sixes I bumped into South African skipper Hansie Cronje. I believe that Hansie was already involved in cricket's worldwide betting scandals, but the extent has not been fully discovered; probably never will be. It was many months before the first whiff of the match-fixing scandal was sensed, but in retrospect, I would be surprised if it didn't go back far longer than we currently know. It was rumoured that the infamous Mukesh Gupta, the key player in the controversy, was in our hotel reception on more than one occasion in Hong Kong.

I'd known Cronje from the 1980s when he would come and stay in Birmingham with Allan Donald; they were best pals. Cronje played a part in Allan becoming a great of the sport. These two literally made a pact through a desire for success, both at home with Free State and later South Africa. They achieved much under Hansie`s leadership, establishing their country as a world force.

Cronje also played in the English leagues in the late 80s, eventually playing county and Test cricket. We played with and against each other several times and I have to say that when the news about match-fixing came out I felt certain it was a mistake. I was sure he was innocent. He let a lot of people down. I know Allan was more shocked than anyone. Outraged, in fact.

The Singapore Sixes was different. The first thing that struck me about Singapore was its cleanliness. Everything appeared to be under control, from the excellent public transport to stringent law and order. Just before the tournament a local priest received several lashings as a new birching law was brought into force, but the result was that the streets felt unusually safe. The trip also afforded an opportunity to spend time with Andy Moles' dad on his boat sailing around on the Great China Sea.

The other thing I remember most about that Sixes were how harsh the umpires were with the bowlers. Conditions were so in favour of the batsmen that there were times when the whole thing was a bit of a farce. The rules restricted where captains could place fielders, so with only two men allowed on each side of the wicket to save runs it was desperately tough to try and contain international batsmen.

As it happened we ended up winning the tournament. That surprised a few people. Winning the Singapore Sixes won't go down in the *Guinness Book of Records* as an achievement, but it was an important and pleasing victory anyway. Competing against top level players from all Test-playing nations was damn hard in that sort of searing heat, especially for bowlers. People often underestimate the importance of the competition; England didn't even enter a side in the Commonwealth Games, but I believe it could, if well marketed, prove to be almost as successful as Twenty20.

Singapore didn't seem to sleep. It was wonderful. Karaoke bars were highly popular at the time and there was no shortage of people willing to get up in front of others and show off their lack of singing ability.

Ex-pats living in Singapore seemed to have a ball. One guy who looked after us picked us up in a new BMW which had just cost him £250,000 after taxes. My ex-father-in-law had just bought the identical car in the UK for £58,000. My friend took me to a few of the night spots where, upon arrival, he told me 2,000 women would run at us when we entered the main area; he wasn't lying.

The following morning, whilst walking to the ground, I passed the markets where only a few hours earlier I had been playing late night dominoes in the company of West Indian fast bowler Sylvester Clarke. I walked past the hustle and bustle on to the famous Singapore Cricket Club gates. The first thing I saw upon my arrival was 'Clarkie' bowling; he delivered an over of outrageous pace, several balls nearly breaking the batsmen's toes. This guy's preparation was not as important to him as it was to others. Had his career spanned the decade after it actually did, he'd have been a huge star as he coincided with the likes of Holding and Garner and so found international opportunites limited. As it was he tragically passed away in his early 40s, just like his fellow Bajan, Malcolm Marshall.

The opportunity to travel has been one of the greatest benefits of my career. There's nothing like it in terms of broadening the mind and learning about the world. A great deal of the ideas and inspiration behind my current work have come from what I've seen on my travels. Those South African townships were particularly eye-opening places, but my experiences in Argentina and Zimbabwe were no less revealing.

I flew into Buenos Aires in 1983. I had a deal with the Argentine Cricket Union to play, coach and generally spread the gospel of cricket. My apartment in the Belgrano district of the city was to have advantages for a 19 year-old. The Falklands war between England and Argentina still loomed large in the memory and life was occasionally difficult, especially when talk of the Argentine warship named The Belgrano, which was sunk in the war, came up. I hadn't realised that the country was suppressed and I hadn't fully appreciated its recent history. The war had affected the lives of many people and there were times when being white and having long, blond hair and an ear-ring caused me to be viewed with some suspicion.

The pace of life in Buenos Aires was contagious, but Argentina as a whole was in total crisis. Years of poor leadership had seen huge rises in inflation and food and other necessities increased in price daily. Local pesos became worthless. Fortunately I was paid in U.S. dollars so could have the life I wanted. I mixed with young Embassy staff and enjoyed a privileged existence.

I never found it hard to resist the cocaine that was all too prevalent. One day I remember two guys dumped a million dollars worth of it in the street and just walked off. There was so much Colombian cocaine floating around, it was easier to lose a million dollars worth than contemplate doing time in a South American jail. It was as common as cappuccino, and cheaper.

Others didn't find it so easy to say no. Diego Maradona used to visit the New York City nightclub in Buenos Aires every couple of weeks and, eventually, developed an addiction for the drug. He would arrive in the club with a large entourage and pick out women to be brought to him. And there are a lot of beautiful women in the city. Maradona's addiction almost killed him but he was motivated to recover by the thought of missing out on seeing his daughters grow up. I can understand that.

Often in Buenos Aires I would go and witness the Argentinean mothers who had lost children standing in silence at Plaza de Mayo. These ladies would be holding placards containing pictures of their missing and kidnapped children. Between 1976 and 1983 over 30,000 civilians simply disappeared. A country run by military and police regimes abducted people in the street and then dropped them out over the Atlantic Ocean or into the River Plate from 35,000 feet on death flights. Many washed up on the beaches of nearby Uruguay. Stories of torture were also common. Often people were taken to Esma, the Naval school near the River Plate soccer stadium. Years later, the mass graves are still being discovered. Esma still stands, only now as a museum to honour "the desaparecido", the disappeared.

Since 1979 only 23 men, women and children who disappeared have been recovered alive. 450 children have been identified and found living with military families unable to conceive children themselves. Years later the editor of the *Buenos Aires Herald* said, "Argentina doesn't have the full story of why suddenly you had a coup that made people vanish off the face of the earth". This was the Argentina I entered and, by the time I left, I felt I had seen enough. I enjoyed the place but was pleased to be moving on.

It wasn't the only place I visited in South America. Uruguay, Paraguay and Peru proved well interesting and more than eye-opening. I took the opportunity to go to Brazil, where the poverty in parts of Rio de Janeiro was quite shocking. Children without shoes and dressed in rags roamed in groups. Child prostitution was rife. The "favelas" (slums) were some of the worst places; despite this there was little crime in these areas. Rio drug lords make sure there isn't.

The police are no better. Their method of dealing with the street children was simply elimination. There's no need to spend money on orphanages if there aren't any orphans. It has since been acknowledged that child murder was a regular occurrence.

Probably the most shocking moment of my life came in Brazil. It was four o'clock one morning and I came across a side street being hosed down. It had clearly been awash with blood. Meanwhile, a group of men were loading metal boxes into trucks. The girl accompanying me quickly led me away: "bodies" she explained. Between 1987 and 2001 more children died on the streets of Rio than did in the entire Israel/Palestine conflict in the same period. Over 600 street kids are known to have died from gunfire in 1998 alone.

Brazil is a place of such contrasts. On the beaches the beautiful people play and the Brazilian love of life shines through. But Christ the Redeemer, towering high above us on Corcovada Peak, sees a lot more than the carnivals and parties.

A little later in life I was delighted to try and help raise some funds for these children. Led Zeppelin guitarist Jimmy Page was shocked when he visited Rio and pledged both his time and money to help. His large donation to Task Brazil enabled the charity to buy a plot of land in the area. 'Casa Jimmy' now provides a safe home for children who other-wise would be in great danger.

I captained Jimmy's cricket team - a pretty eclectic bunch of musicians, film producers and actors - in a few games to raise funds and will be happy to do anything more in the future.

Jimmy empathised with what I was trying to achieve. He spoke of a gig Led Zeppelin played outside L.A. in Inglewood. Afterwards the band heard that the local kids from the 'hood were high-jacking the cars of white kids as they left. They stole their concert t-shirts and any other memorabilia they may have picked-up. And, of course, their cash.

It's funny; Jimmy told me he was 14 when he realised what he wanted to do for a living. I was about the same age when I knew that I was going to be a cricketer. What a luxury. In Rio, or countless other places around the globe, 14-year-old kids can't dream of the future; they're just trying to survive in the present.

I had almost exactly the same conversation with the lead singer of The Who, Roger Daltrey. He reckoned he knew he was going to be a singer from the age of five, when he entertained guests at a wedding by singing with the band. Later, in the U.S., I was struck by the contrast in these aspirations and those of some of the kids living in the ghetto areas. Some of them actually told me their dream was to be a crack dealer!

There were elements of the same sort of practices in Zimbabwe. Even before I went I had been warned that it was a country in decline. A guy I knew who had been with Bob Marley for the Independence Day celebrations in 1980 told me that Bob would be turning in his grave if he could see what Mugabe was doing to the country. Certainly the country has regressed. Since Mugabe took over the average life expectancy in Zimbabwe has fallen to just 37 years. Infant mortality has soared and more than two million people in the country are living with Aids. Many fear that Zimbabwe could turn into this decade's Rwanda.

The closest the Warwickshire team came to Mugabe on our pre-season tour was as we were driving back to Harare after a game. Suddenly our cars were effectively shoved off the road as Mugabe's motorcade sped past us in a blaze of sirens and flashing lights. It was intimidating.

Mugabe's presidential house overlooks the Harare Sports Club ground. Heavily armed guards protect him at all times, while the road approaching his home is covered in devices designed to blow-up the tyres of any vehicle.

We were also introduced to the former leader of the then Rhodesia, Ian Smith. He required no such security and, after the game, jumped into an old Renault 5 motor car and drove himself home. One of life's humble people. I asked Smith about the time his son Alec had brought Arthur Kanodereka, the treasurer of the ANC, directly into his presidential and family home. At the time it was a brave move, guerrilla warfare against blacks was more common. It is not every day you meet a guy like Ian Smith and a fascinating conversation took place whilst we watched our game unfold, talking about independence, times in Zimbabwe's history and its possible future. Smith had obviously experienced some worries with his son, who had been quite a heavy user of marijuana. But Smith senior said he had been, and always would be, "his rock".

I also spoke to some to of the people at the sharp end of life in Zimbabwe. My Warwickshire team-mate Trevor Penney had been brought up in Zimbabwe and had a couple of domestic helpers in his home, Agnes and Albert. From conversations with them, I gathered that there is no future for the country. They told me that inflation was making it impossible to even afford a loaf of bread and how lucky they were to live in a house - provided by Penney - with such basics as running water. Inflation currently runs at somewhere around 1,700%. When we toured there a house with a tennis court and pool cost 200,000 Zimbabwe dollars. Now that would barely buy you a dozen bricks.

One of the more surprising characters I met out there was Test umpire Russell Tiffin. He had seen action during the Rhodesian war and had experienced far more stressful events than a cricket match would ever throw at him. He was as hard as nails. One day he asked me to try and hurt him by pulling the skin under his arm. Throughout the exercise Russ showed no signs of feeling pain. Two days later the area was black with bruising. He told me that pain is in the mind.

There were some amazing characters in the Warwickshire dressing room, too. One such guy was Jamaican Alpheus Sam, who once told me that he lost his virginity to a chicken. It had happened back in the West Indies when he was a youngster. I'm told it died during the activity; its final sounds being "chuck, chuck, chuck". The feathered one was then by all accounts deposited over the fence into the neighbours' garden. I just hope they didn't eat it. I've no idea if he was telling me the truth. Pretty weird thing to make up, though.

I was no different. Well, a bit different; my relationship with chickens has been strictly platonic. Just good friends. I first took the field (as a substitute fielder) for Warwickshire's first team about a month after my 15th birthday. I believe I'm the youngest ever to do so. For the next couple of decades I made my living playing cricket. Then, as a result of my own foolishness and some intransigent action from my sport's governing body, it was over. There was no immediate work, little qualifications. Apparently, given the circumstances, little future.

I owe the Professional Cricketers' Association - the players' union - much. They later put a roof over my head and helped with finding the funding to support my community activity aspirations in which I'd shown an interest. In reality they could not have done more to help me and I will be eternally grateful. I know they've helped a lot of other players too. I don't think I'm out of order saying that for a few they've been the difference between life or death.

The players' union are well meaning, increasingly well-organised and professional. There are, however, a number who are simply ex-players who may lack real life and work experience, and this can cause problems. At times I worried about the relevant experience of some of the representatives who they sent around the counties to warn players of the dangers of dabbling in any type of drugs. I also doubted people's ability to keep personal issues confidential. I know from experience that deeply personal matters slipped out to journalists that should never have been commented upon. One journalist rang me and, in amongst polite conversation, confronted me with specific issues that he should never have known about. Once that sort of character knew it was difficult to make progress. Especially as he was the ruthless, sly type.

Since I played my last game in 1996, everything's changed in English cricket. Throughout my career it was obvious we were asked to perform on too many consecutive days. Not just that: with the travel thrown in, it led to a frantic schedule without any fear of relegation. In this period, Surrey's Sylvester Clarke and Monty Lynch once turned up at New Road, Worcester when they should have been performing at Swansea. Life was a constant criss-cross of motorways. A fixture card in your glove box, enough spare kit in the boot, and you were on your way.

Playing contracts of the past limited player/coach bonding time once the season ended. Nowadays, a 10-month a year contract adds professionalism; player analysis is 100 per cent better, the four-month extra employment and monitoring time should lead to continued improvement in the quality of play. Previous generations could, if they wished, sit on their backsides for the duration of an off-season, only to surface in April, suddenly reborn as a professional cricketer.

Had two divisions been in existence earlier it would have killed off the common act of batting for statistical benefit. Most teams had their bean counters. Cricket-playing accountants. They don't survive in a thriving atmosphere but, in relegation-free leagues, too many selfish players could find a niche. There were a few bean counters at Edgbaston; it coincided with a period where we won absolutely nothing. Nowadays the only possible place to bean count and exist is in the lower professional league bowels.

The more recent introduction of two divisions should have taught people to force the pace, to make things happen. Forcing the pace is playing for the team, not your average. The team will benefit, either in sessions, short-term or over a season. If you can't adapt your game to help the team like that, it's the equivalent of a premier league soccer player being unable to kick with both feet.

Counties twenty years ago had the luxury of a fast bowlers' open market. It created a workplace where batsmen regularly faced the likes of Roberts, Clarke, Garner, Holding, Marshall, Ambrose, Walsh, Bishop and Patterson. Performers like Wayne Daniel couldn't command a place in the awesome West Indian side of the time, the same applied to Davis, Grey and Ezra Moseley. You had to learn, perform and try to win games all at the same time. Damn hard. Sometimes, you had to do it for 27 days on the run.

In one game, Hampshire's Malcolm Marshall hit me four times. Each body blow, if inflicted in a normal workplace, would have led to an instant sick note, a long time off, no questions asked. I believe on-field antics from this era led to the term "mental disintegration". It was harsh.

In my early career a percentage of Warwickshire supporters felt Bob Willis didn't try hard enough when he came back from England duty to play for the county. Yet Willis wanted to win trophies more than most. A big atmosphere brought the best out in him. Knee problems probably cost him at least 100 Test wickets. That he finished with 325 wickets was a major personal feat. Given help and some form of embryonic central contract, it could have risen to around the 450 to 500 mark.

Of other English fast bowlers, Botham would be hostile with the ball. He was as strong as an ox with even greater reserves of spirit and determination. Graham Dilley was damn rapid, too. English cricket has always produced bowlers who could get the ball through, it's just the fixture card went against them in the 80s and 90s and the man management in operation often resembled instructions from Captain Mainwaring. Forget the workloads of previous generations of cricketers; they mostly took place where no one-day competitions existed. The game and expectations were different, life was different.

Ashes winner Steve Harmison has benefited from a far better monitoring system. Rather than being thrown out

MACO

This hook shot off Malcolm Marshall landed in the upper tier of the stands, the area now known as the Executive Club at Edgbaston. I can't say that I was always so successful against Marshall. He was the very best. His extreme pace was one thing, but he could also move the ball both ways with ease. He was an inspiration. What's not always appreciated is his spirit. He had an enormous appetite for life and gave his all whether playing for Hampshire, Barbados, Natal or the West Indies. We socialised every time we were in the same city and I considered him a friend. I once batted against him at Bournemouth after spending several hours in the Royal Motor Yacht club bar; an experience in itself. Three hours earlier we had been told that play for the day was washed out - then the dreaded phone call came through: we were to restart shortly and I would be on strike against him. When the moment of truth came I walked out to open the batting when Macco sidled up to me and said, "Don't worry, Smitty Boy, this won't take long". He was as good as his word. After several minutes I was on my way - initially walking in the wrong direction, away from the pavilion. Try facing objects hurled straight at you at 90mph plus when you are three sheets to the wind!
On one occasion during another fixture against Hampshire, Marshall drove from Portsmouth one evening to collect a friend from Heathrow airport. On the way he had an accident and rolled his BMW on the motorway; a terrifying and potentially deadly experience. Yet the next morning he was back on the field, bowling against us as if nothing were had happened. There aren't many who wouldn't have taken the day off. It really is a miracle that Hampshire won so little in the decade or so he was with them.
I reckon I had one of the last conversations with Marshall before he was informed of the seriousness of his condition. We were chatting at Edgbaston as the West Indies played a World Cup warm-up game against Warwickshire in May 1999. He was tremendously supportive of my early ideas to use sport as a vehicle for improving the lives of underprivileged or dispossessed kids and had urged me to make it a success. He then took the short journey up the road to Birmingham's Nuffield Hospital where he was informed about the reason for the stomach pains he had been experiencing; cancer of the colon. It proved the bullet of fate. He died in the November. Like the word 'genius' - the word 'tragedy' is over-used in sport, but on this occasion no other descriptions fit. He was 41 years-old and with a huge amount left to offer.

onto the park simply because he's fast and the fixture card dictates there's games to be played, he has been looked after. Unlike Willis.

The greatest change in the last 20 years is the advent of central playing contracts. Their arrival protects the best players. Botham was seriously injured when forced into playing for Somerset in a friendly against Cambridge University - and this in an era where his competitors, the likes of Imran Khan, played virtually no domestic cricket in Pakistan. Can't imagine 'Freddie' Flintoff repeating that trick.

English supporters of Botham's genre were lucky to see as much of Beefy's colossal talent as they did. 'Beef' hit the splice hard. He had swing, pace and a golden arm. It was a fault in the system that stuffed him, with his preferred style of important match preparation, his skill and brain would've enabled him to recreate heroics even longer. I haven't even mentioned Botham's batting; he'd empty bars when he walked to the crease, this after he'd filled them with his match presence. This perhaps is what English first-class cricket misses.

Lancashire's Andrew Flintoff could do a similar job nowadays, but he's tragically rarely seen, our draw cards are constantly absent. It's a big problem for those trying to sell the new version of English first-class cricket, and shouldn't be hidden from the punter.

Early in my career I was playing at Old Trafford. I witnessed Lancashire skipper John Abrahams having a big dig at opening batsman Graeme Fowler. Fowler, an England regular, turned to me and said, "I've played in six Tests this summer, I'm knackered."

In the present era, Fowler wouldn't even have been at the ground. He would have benefited from the sort of cushion given to Marcus Trescothick, although even he became a caualty of the high intensity of professional sport. Seeingly superhuman Andrew 'Freddie' Flintoff played in just one first-class match for Lancashire in 2006. Fowler's Lancastrian team-mate Michael Atherton took breaks between Test matches. Now Michael Vaughan appears like a cricketing supernova for Yorkshire: two kids at a Test match during the Ashes summer of 2005 told me Vaughan plays for England, they didn't know he had any affiliation with Yorkshire. In comparison, Willis, when England's skipper, would often have to travel back to Edgbaston and immediately be expected to bowl fast for us.

ECB Chairman David Morgan recently said that he favours a return to a single league and a minimum 120 overs per day. One wonders how much three-day cricket he ever watched. He certainly never played it. A return to zero relegation would put the game back decades. During a Championship fixture between Warwickshire and Middlesex at Lord's in June 1984, our opening batsmen returned to the crease at 8.20pm to start our second innings on that particular day. The ground was empty, the performers in the middle only because previous generations had it that way. That's how it had always been. Earlier in this day I'd scored the highest individual score of the game with 80, becoming the only man to pass 50 in the match. Afterwards the BBC's Nick Owen interviewed me on the Lord's balcony.

The promotion and relegation system we have now must stay; it creates more drama, more passion, more fight - and more results.

English cricket is getting it right. The national side benefits from controlling the England squad's activity when not on duty. Twenty20 has rejuvenated it, brought in a new audience. It is, however, only an extension of something played at every club ground around this country, dressed up with music and colored clothing.

No one has reinvented the wheel. Kerry Packer came close 30 years ago with the changes he precipitated in World Series Cricket, but it's essentially the same thing. As for the carnival atmosphere of Twenty20, it's great to see, of course it is. But I look back at the men who ran the game in the early 80s and the way they drove away West Indian supporters who used to delight in blowing horns, playing drums, knocking cans and encouraging their team. Now, 25 years later, the same type of people are doing everything they can to fill our grounds again with as much noise, spirit and off-field activity as they can muster. How ironic!

Wasted?

Coming Down

I CONSIDER MYSELF VERY fortunate to have played cricket with Brian Charles Lara. So many performers leave their sport with little or no silverware. There is nothing worse in sport than shattered hopes and unfulfilled dreams. We at Warwickshire, however, were different.

'Persevere and Triumph' they say. Well, we did that. A few of us at Warwickshire had to persevere through less happy times for a decade or more beforehand.

Lara's arrival at Edgbaston provided the catalyst for us to go on and achieve unprecedented success. Warwickshire's treble successes in this era are now part of folklore.

Like many people I'd watched Brian's brilliant perform-ances for the West Indies against England in the Caribbean over the English winter of 1993-94. A few days after Lara had scored a hundred in the third Test my phone rang. On the other end is a mate who lives in Barbados telling me that news on the island was rife that Lara was signing a deal to play for Warwickshire this coming summer. This guy had once told me about seeing the 13 year-old Lara play. He'd said Lara, who he described as a "little guy", had walked to the crease with a cap sitting on an afro; this fix-ture had been an adult game of high standard. Lara tore all the bowlers apart. The innings was all the more memorable because Brian was so small and slight. My friend was as chuffed as me that Lara was on his way to us. "Watch the master closely" was his parting comment.

In April 1994 Warwickshire vice-chairman Tony Cross unexpectedly departed for Barbados. By hook or by crook we signed our man, and just in time. Within days Brian had re-written the game's record books by breaking the high-est individual Test score. Had Lara and his agent Jonathan

Barnett stalled a few days his Warwickshire earnings would have trebled.

It so nearly didn't happen. Manoj Prabhakar was our original overseas signing - counties were allowed only one player eligible to play for a country other than England in their squad at the time - but supposedly turned up injured. How injured he was is open to speculation, though it's true that he did have a scar on his ankle from a fairly recent operation. Once Lara became available I think the committee were pretty keen to get rid of Prabhakar, anyway. He was set a fitness test that a leopard couldn't have passed! It suited me as Prabhakar was an all-rounder and he might have pushed me out of the side in some games.

The Warwickshire squad had just returned from our pre-season tour of Zimbabwe when news of Lara's signing filtered through. We sat in the Edgbaston committee rooms watching live coverage of the Test in Antigua. Everyone willed Brian to break that Sir Garfield Sobers' record of 365. TV cameras were filming us watching him. Lara was now within a week of joining us and the thought of performing in the same side as this super-talented individual was among the most exciting thoughts of my career. I don't believe I was the only one thinking that either; all of us, his future team-mates, sat glued to the wide screen.

Later, when he joined us he told me that the day he passed the record he played a round of golf first thing in the morning. He was 320 not out overnight but couldn't sleep so felt that it would help him relax. His other consideration was to take an early morning plane ride around Antigua. It's a good thing he chose golf, the plane he was most likely to travel on actually crashed killing those on board

When he arrived in May 1994 we weren't disappointed; time and again he annihilated bowling attacks. Every team would bring on their best bowlers against him, only to be repeatedly smashed to the boundary fences. No one could control Brian on the pitch. He was on a different level. Our season gathered momentum. We were exciting to watch; our crowds grew and our expectations skyrocketed.

It wasn't just Lara, of course. We had the world's premier coach in Bob Woolmer, while Dermot Reeve was streets ahead of other captains. Add to this squad Brian Lara, a hungry one at that, and you had a team worth watching. Every person involved had a passion, a real drive and spirit that eventually took things to unmatched heights.

Warwickshire were only to lose on four occasions over our triumphant summer. Taking into account how many games we played, 43, it's a pretty amazing statistic. We rose 15 places in the table that year - a record - and played a different style to the rest; always aggressive but just as importantly with a sense of humour never far from the surface. Nearly every squad member became a happening cricketer. Everybody had to add urgency to their game just to be considered for selection. It was a breath of fresh air.

Lara scored hundred after hundred. He became the first man to score seven first-class centuries in eight innings and equalled Don Bradman's record of passing 1,000 runs in his seventh innings of the season. In all he scored more than 2,000 at very close to a run a ball. Then we witnessed the genius breaking Hanif Mohammad's world record score of 499 when we played Durham. When the Trinidadian drove a half-volley for four to bring his score to 501 it was a supercharged moment. The hairs stood up on the back of my neck. Our coach Bob Woolmer is probably the only person who witnessed both innings. Having been brought up in India, he had been lucky enough to see Hanif`s record-breaking innings 36 years earlier.

When Lara was on his way to 501, word spread through the country like wildfire about what was taking place at Edgbaston. By all accounts Birmingham was buzzing with talk about what was happening. People left work early to catch some of the action; newspaper salesmen shouted Lara updates; the roads around the stadium became gridlocked.

Nearly a decade later, Australian Matt Hayden smashed a marathon 380 without being dismissed against Zimbabwe in Perth. Lara's Test record was gone. The Trinidadian's response was almost immediate. Within months he lifted the world record to 400, again in Antigua, again against England. It reminded observers that the man's in a different league, capable of virtually any feat. His inner mental strength is phenomenal; it's why he's achieved what he has. Remember his own career coincided with a huge downward turn in West Indian standards of play and achievement. Australian captain Steve Waugh got it right when he said: "He's a good player against average bowling sides and a great one against formidable attacks. But when harrassed into a corner by his own brinkmanship, or if he's targeted, he elevates himself into a genius."

I first encountered a young Lara during the 1991 West Indies tour of England. Viv Richards, captaining his country on his last trip abroad before retirement, asked if I'd bowl at his batsmen before the Edgbaston Test. Together with Ian Bishop, Malcolm Marshall and Curtley Ambrose I bowled at B.C. for half-an-hour on a wicket offering more than a little assistance. Brian played the first 15 minutes with perfect defence. The following 15 produced an incredible demonstration of his ability to dismantle attacks. Every shot in the book came out, full-blooded drives, delicate cuts and hooks, all hit with enormous power.

West Indies tour coach Wes Hall shouted out "last round". Lara, Marshall, Bishop and Ambrose and I agree that fourteen runs off the next four balls wins the contest for the batter. I bowl the first ball, which is struck back past me with the speed of an express train; four runs. Marshall was next up, bowling an identical ball - the result is the same. The pressure is now on Ambrose to deliver the perfect delivery. He did so, as if his life depended on it, pitching the ball short, so it reared up, aiming at Lara's right temple. Yet Brian's lightening fast reflexes and speed of eye combined to help him dispatch the ball the best part of eighty yards, disappearing over the rooftops on to the Pershore Road with a perfectly executed hook shot. I glanced to my left upon hearing Ian Bishop shout "Murder!" a great description of the scene. Ambrose was the world's premier fast bowler, and Lara, then, an almost unknown young batsmen. It was to take another three years before he registered the highest individual scores in the history of our sport and became a household name. Indeed, on that 1991 trip Lara actually asked if he could go back to Trinidad as, "You're not going to pick me for the big games." A few months later B.C. proved his point when scoring 277 in Sydney against Australia.

In that 1994 season I witnessed first hand, both on and off the pitch, how special Brian was. The experience changes you, seeing how simple thought patterns brought about chaos for opponents. Lara's advice and theories made the words of wisdom spouted by the many manual-toting coaches sound redundant and hollow in comparison.

These things that were happening for Brian Lara and his new team don't happen every day. His life had changed forever within a few weeks. He was just 24 years-old and everyone wanted a piece of him. I remember going back to his Edgbaston apartment at the end of a day's play. His answer machine was full. His fax machine had used a huge roll of paper. Due to enormous success with us and the West Indian team, Brian's mailbag regularly stacked up taller than his dressing room chair.

Whilst our summer unfolded people looked for cracks to appear. Lara was said to be a bad influence. Some said he wasn't a team man and was only there to make money. I beg to differ. All people have to be selfish at times. I wouldn't say Brian was, but too many people made demands on his time. If he didn't respond positively to these people he was criticised. At his young age, and without much help from a club that was ill-prepared for such success, he was put in some impossible situations. Lara cared.

During a practice net session at Edgbaston a particular woman became the topic of conversation. When someone admitted he'd spent time with her, but didn't love the girl at all, Lara sighed. "Doesn't anyone love anyone any more?" he asked. He was different to most people, especially most men.

We have all been late once or twice in our life. Lara's schedule was far busier than most. He was once caught in a motorway traffic jam due to roadworks and was late getting to the ground at Taunton for a one-day game. It didn't matter, it rained and he was ready to take to the field when we finally did start. The fact he was late for a television interview greatly annoyed a journalist, however, and led to much criticism. Obviously the critics on this particular day thought a young Trinidadian, only a few months in the country, should have known the back routes! One reporter ranted: "In 40 years of following this sport I've never seen such behavior." Complete bollocks.

Within the structure of a team there are better ways to punish inappropriate behaviour. On my first-class debut, Andy Lloyd, a future Warwickshire captain, failed to turn up until play had been underway for an hour-and-a-half in a match against Cambridge University. Bob Willis made the guilty party field at fine leg for hours, meaning he had to run from one end of the ground to the other for over after over. That was punishment enough.

You can criticise anything and anyone if you dig deep enough. I can't think of a player who was never late at some stage of his career. It happens, but never makes the news. Little was written or said about all the positive things he was doing off the field. For example, Lara personally organised our end of season party, buying all the alcohol and food, paying for a D.J. etc. B.C. did lots of things that others didn't. No-one acknowledged that.

Much was written about Lara's input on and off the field. You may have read that he was unpopular within the dressing room. It's not how I saw things. The Trinidadian had started the day of our Benson and Hedges final by giving a memorable team talk in our changing room at Lord's. It was inspiring. Everyone gained from his presence. Most importantly, I suppose, he put backsides on seats.

When poor overnight weather delayed the start of a Championship match at Lord's, Brian gathered the top six in our batting order after we had practiced in the indoor facilities. We spent the time talking of what motivates individuals. Perhaps international honours, fame, money - everyone is different. He said he was motivated by his father. Although he'd died, Brian felt he was watching over him. He wanted his father to be proud of his achievements. I believe Lara was with us all the way that season, but immense outside pressures sometimes gave the impression he was not.

We shared a great respect for Sir Garfield Sobers. Who doesn't, you might ask? But both of us had enjoyed the opportunity to get to know him a little bit and both were impressed by the man. I had coached a fair bit in Australia with Sobers and had watched as he found a way to impart his immense wisdom to thousands of kids of different ages and abilities. One day he was trying to explain a technical issue about batting. After a while he went in front of the bowling machine and asked for it to be set to 85 mph. He then gave a perfect demonstration of his point, playing every ball with the middle of the bat. It would have been impressive enough from a current player, but Sobers was in his mid 50s by then and wearing neither gloves or pads. He was just a class above.

I was lucky enough to gain an unusual insight into Sobers' awesome sporting ability. After sharing a bottle of brandy one night, he showed me how he could drive golf balls with unerring accuracy. The amazing thing about it was that he hit two balls with the same, left-handed club; the first one using a right-handed stance and the second left-handed. Both balls zipped perfectly straight for very similar distances. Talents like Sobers don't come along very often.

Whilst we were in London, Lara had agreed to give up his time to promote his home island of Trinidad at a function in Leicester Square. Over 2,000 people gathered, each in some way had a direct link with the tiny island. Brian's speech was based around his pride of being Trinidadian and how much the country's development meant to him.

After the formalities he stayed for ages, chatting and signing all sorts of memorabilia thrust in his direction. This took place during a time when, if you believed what was being printed, you would think he was the most mercenary person on earth. Yet that night, like many others, he gave his time for free.

Leaving this West End venue we walked through the crowd. The place was packed with soccer fans. Despite the difference between the two sports and their supporters, Lara was greeted with total respect. His achievements demand no less. It's a shame others who followed and commented on our own sport didn't feel the same way. At that time or now.

One night during this Lord's game I hooked up with an old school friend now working for Sanctuary Records. We met up in a restaurant in Soho. After a few hours catching up, she and I jumped in a cab to Fulham. After a night in various venues we ended up at a house party. I departed at 7am. Within hours I was batting with Lara at the home of cricket. We put on a partnership of 95, of which my share was 65; it felt easy, despite the preparation. Now, whenever I see the musicians who were with me the night before they say they don't know how I could have played professional sport after the evening we'd had. It's laughable, yet shows the faith I had in my ability and talent, especially at this stage in life. It also shows the lengths I was prepared to go to in order to have a good time! Life, after all, was for living.

During our partnership Lara announced where he would hit every delivery off England spinner John Emburey's next over. The first five deliveries all disappeared, either striking or fractionally missing the advertising boards he'd targeted. The last delivery he told me would go "distance". Picture, if you will, the pavilion at Lord's - in each top corner there is a turret with a flag. The last delivery Emburey delivered struck the top left flag, care of Brian's 2lb 6 oz bat. Only once in cricketing history has a player hit the ball over the pavilion. Lara would have cleared it by miles if it hadn't struck the pole; it was a monstrous hit. Check it out next time you visit the ground; some people get a bus to travel that far. Lara described the shot as the most effortless he had ever played. Brian would have collected £50,000 from a London-based insurance company but for that thin bit of wood. When I told him, he smiled. £50k missed by an inch.

Too much was asked of Lara that summer. There were times when he was simply exhausted, but was forced to play. One televised Sunday game at Northampton springs to mind. 20 minutes before the start I was told Lara's knee wasn't great and that he also had a headache after sustaining a blow on the helmet from West Indian paceman Curtly Ambrose when batting the previous day. Lara can't play, fair enough. If you looked at the facts and understood the demands, then you would see that the guy had hardly had a second off the pitch over the previous few months. He just needed a day off.

Yet five minutes later a discussion started in the middle involving our captain, coach, vice-captain and several members of our committee. Perhaps most relevant, however, was the presence in the middle of the pitch of Sky TV officials voicing opinions about viewers' requirements. In the end, B.C. was forced to play. In no other occupation would it occur. Most people would have just phoned in sick if put under such pressure. In sports such as football, managers like Arsène Wenger and Sir Alex Ferguson make great capital out of resting their star players when they deem it necessary.

At the end of the season I called Brian on his mobile. My benefit year was coming up and I asked if he would sign 100 bats on my behalf. He explained that he was in London with no plans to return to Edgbaston, but he would see what he could do.

24 hours later he called to say the bats had been signed. He'd done every one. Don't believe everything you hear about Brian Lara; as someone who played a season of cricket with him and spent plenty of time in his company off the pitch, I would say he was a great team player and a great man.

Perhaps the stories of his selfishness and aloofness can be put down to jealousy. Lara was successful, confident and good-looking. His great friend from childhood, Dwight Yorke, was often around and the two are high profile figures. Women couldn't get enough of them. Some lesser men wanted to knock them down to size.

Lara's time with Warwickshire was not without controversy. During a County Championship match versus
Northamptonshire in June, Brian and our skipper Dermot
Reeve exchanged words over a catch that umpire Alan
Jones disallowed. The West Indian ended up swearing at
the skipper in a well-publicised dispute, which brought him
heavy criticism.

In reality it was no big deal. These things happen during
a season, particularly if you question an individual's integrity.
The verbal clash should never have happened; Lara had
caught the ball, the batsman was clearly out. Despite the
publicity, any verbal confrontation did not disrupt the
match-winning efforts of the side. Everyone still rooted for
everyone.

For the record, Lara top scored with 177 in this game.
He played Curtly Ambrose's fierce spells with great determination and, for the rest of us; it was exhilarating viewing
as the two proud superstars enjoyed a rare public confrontation. Lara's pride won that day, but don't knock
Ambrose's effort. He gave it plenty.

Perhaps those who took delight in knocking the
Trinidadian at every opportunity should reflect a bit more
before criticising. I played 486 first team games for
Warwickshire and heard much worse cussing than came
out that day. Lara was not the only player to tell Dermot
where to get off. In fact, you would have to cull the earth
of trees to print every event where Derm was told to "Fuck
Off". If Joe Soap swore, no one gave a damn, but if it was
Lara, it made headlines.

Dermot and I had been on the Lord's groundstaff
together in 1981. I would always rather have him in my
team than not; but as an opponent you would want to take
a baseball bat to him. Reeve's humour was good and
clever; he often diffused tense situations that way. It was
clever captaincy.

As teenagers we were on the Lord's groundstaff
together during the summer of 1981. Mick Jagger bought
a handful of scorecards from us during the Lord's Test that
year. Australian Tim Zoerher and Kiwi Martin Crowe were

also there. Crowe was in a different class to the rest of us. In fact he was ahead of most of the professionals we saw while we operated the scoreboard. I shared a room with him in our home just off Hampstead High Street. He's the cousin of the actor, Russell Crowe.

Martin was a good guy once you got to know him, but he could be pretty intense. During one flare-up at Lord's, one of the other groundstaff lads accused him of being selfish. He replied, "I haven't come here to make friends." Single-minded determination made him into one of the very best batsmen the game has seen. Maybe there was a bit of Russell in Martin.

He showed that tough side one day when we played a game against the army. I was bowling pretty quickly and the army batsmen were backing away from the ball. "Running away from a piece of leather, you weak bastard," Crowe would mutter at them from the slips. I guess the incident showed the different sort of courage needed for a life in sport compared to a life as a professional soldier. Later we were within seconds of overhauling their total and winning the game so we asked their skipper if we could push the tea interval back an over. "Certainly not," their captain replied. "It's the army's prerogative." Crowe hit the first ball after tea for four to seal the game and left the pitch with a torrent of abuse towards their skipper.

Like Crowe, both Reeve and Lara were characters who played to win. That was all that was important. Team laughter was never far from the surface as the spirit within the group blossomed. However, plenty of people had an opinion about Reeve as a person. He and I had a few sharp exchanges of words over the years, but then we've shared a lot of amazing experiences together.

He was excellent at evaluating a person's character. Before the Lord's final against Worcestershire in 1994 there were a few who thought I shouldn't be in the team due to some fitness concerns. But Dermot would just ask, "How are you feeling?" and as long as I was positive, I was in. He knew I was a potential match-winner and, as an all-rounder, gave him extra options. By winning the Man of the

Match award as we clinched the Benson & Hedges trophy, I think I proved his judgment spot on.

Dermot had the ability to wind up any opponent. Once we were playing Somerset at Edgbaston and Pakistan leg-spinner Mushtaq Ahmed was bowling. I was at the non-striker's end when Derm started running down the wicket to nearly every ball and shouting out what type of delivery was being bowled. "Leggy", he shouted to one ball. "Oh, the wrong 'un", he said as Mushtaq delivered his googly, or "top spinner; well bowled." He read every ball perfectly and announced it by using his excellent impersonation of Imran Khan. The treatment really got to Mushtaq and it wasn't long before he was withdrawn from the attack.

Later in the season we played the return fixture at Taunton. This rain-affected one-day game looked as if it was going to go down to the wire and Mushy's role was sure to be significant. I was scoring quickly but needed support. Within minutes of Dermot joining me in the middle, however, the direction of the game was set. "Well bowled," he would say after striking Mushy into the river outside the ground. Mushy hated it and it wasn't long before he was on his way down to third man, taking with him his long-sleeved sweater.

It wasn't just spinners Dermot would wind up. West Indian pacemen Curtly Ambrose and Winston Benjamin both resorted to bowling beamers at him after he had man-aged to get under their skin. It was almost like an insult to them that this guy could strike them to the boundary. Curtly completely lost the plot when he was bowling at Dermot; maybe the only time in his career that it happened. He bowled several beamers in a row and, before the start of play the following morning, was forced to apologise.

Dermot used that Imran impression a lot. When Wasim Akram was swinging the ball around corners one time I remember him actually going on to the pitch with a bottle top to hand to the bowler, again talking in his Imran voice all the time. He was clearly indicating that Wasim was gaining swing by unfair methods - maybe even gouging one side of the leather ball so it aged prematurely, and in doing so, making batting many times harder for our team later when the ball reached that condition and reverse swing became possible. Actually Dermot dealt with it in a quite humorous manner. That was fairly typical Dermot, because he wasn't even playing in that game. He was quite happy to wind up Wasim - one of the best fast bowlers in the world - but then he didn't have to face the consequences.

Dermot was quite clever in the way he handled those issues, though. Whenever Wasim or Waqar played at Edgbaston, we made sure that someone would make a big show of videoing their every move on the pitch; the clear implication being that we were trying to catch them ball-tampering. It didn't even matter if the camera was turned on; its very presence acted as a preventative measure.

Reeve was even called into a meeting at Lord's to explain himself after one Championship game. The problem was that he kept running down the wicket against the spinners, kicking the ball and throwing his bat away to ensure it didn't make contact with the ball. I believe he said there was nothing in the rules to say he couldn't!

There were times he annoyed our own players and coaches. Everyone accepted the success, but they couldn't always hack the man. Personally I was a fan. I'd known Derm much longer than the rest of them. People who had been involved at Edgbaston for decades often found his personality intimidating. The fact that Reeve asked questions of long-standing club figures was sometimes seen as a threat. He would suggest dropping senior players to the seconds if they weren't carrying their weight and was not afraid of suggesting that some on the coaching staff were past their sell-by date and needed a refresher course.

There were times he could be selfish, too. Tim Munton, the team's vice-captain, would often have to change his plans after the skipper made himself unavailable for meetings if paid speaking engagements cropped up. It drove Tim nuts at times. He had a wife and two kids to keep happy; Dermot didn't.

Umpires weren't always impressed by him, either. Sometimes a few of them would behave like the old style

schoolmaster; they disliked anyone rocking the boat or rais-
ing issues. We were a noisy, enthusiastic bunch both on and
off the pitch. Umpire Alan Jones once actually asked us to
tone down our encouragement for one of our bowlers.
Dermot asked him why. Maybe the umpire would rather have
us moping about with our arses in our hands like some of
our opponents did. There's zero wrong with encouragement,
it's what makes things tick in the real world. Jones obviously
didn't agree this day.

There was a lot of the Ian Chappell, Aussie-style steel
in Reeve. He had played years of tough cricket down under
in the Englsih winter break and had learned to impose himself. He knew he was an effective player without being a
world-beater and he often played without much flair. What
he did, however, was achieve the best results possible,
both individually and collectively. Unfortunately, this trait
isn't always appreciated. It made rivals jealous.

The other thing people disliked about our leader was
his success with women. Derm knew many women, had
excellent communication skills and, as we all know, a certain type of woman will always be attracted to what's successful and different. He was all those things.

On the whole, though, he was very popular at
Warwickshire. Ask anyone in that team who we wanted
arguing our corner if we were in trouble, and Dermot's
name would be the first to come up. Enough said.

At the end of that record-breaking summer we were
nominated for several awards. A real highlight was being
invited to the BBC Sports Personality Of The Year award
evening in London. We were shortlisted for team of the
year - though we eventually lost out to Wigan rugby league
club, who had won the Challenge Cup for a seventh consecutive year and the League for a sxith - but were delighted
to spend a night in the company of so many sporting legends.

I spent some time chatting to Colonel Stephenson, my
former boss from the time I was on the MCC groundstaff
as a promising young cricketer. We reflected on how useful
my time at Lord's was and how times had changed. He had
been a fine, almost paternal figure for us youngsters away

from home for the first time. We laughed at the times he would bat against us in the nets, placing £1 on his wicket for each time we dismissed him. For boys earning only £48 a week, this money could make all the difference and sometimes I would leave with an extra £5. He was a great man who went out of his way to help people that others might have thought of as unimportant.

This 1994 treble season was one long, fantastic summer. Many of us just happened to peak as players at the same moment and we had enormous confidence in ourselves and our team-mates. We were dominant. Although we sometimes allowed the opposition to reach the brink of victory, we would always find something extra and scrap like hell until we turned the game in our favour. It's what all good units do.

It didn't make us popular, though. We were surprised by the hostility our success aroused in our opponents and their supporters. Eventually I began to question the negative attitude of our detractors; after all we were achieving success and entertaining.

After winning a game at Cardiff the crowd became really nasty. As we ran off, punches were thrown and there was a time I really thought we may be seriously hurt. Standing on the balcony, a full bottle of vodka smashed through the window behind me; it missed me and Andy Moles by a couple of inches.

To make matters worse, the police didn't seem interested. They said that most supporters were fine until they were drunk and when I mentioned that my car had been damaged they said that having a car like mine - a corvette - was "asking for trouble." Perhaps the jealousy extended to the local constabulary.

We enjoyed our rewards, however. Even ten years later there were still dinners to mark the achievement, while the 12 months following the season's end were quite frenetic. One highlight was the side's trip to Buckingham Palace, where we all received a memento from Prince Philip. It was fascinating to catch a view of the inside of the palace; something I could hardly have dreamed about as a kid growing up in Newcastle. The Prince was impressive. He stopped to chat to every player and seemed knowledgeable and interested. After the presentations in the Palace cinema, we had our photos taken both with the Prince and the three trophies in the gardens at the back and then in front of the Palace. The team finally departed Buckingham Palace for a celebratory meal in London, though we were to return at the end of 1995 when we won another couple of trophies.

Another highlight of that treble season was a victory parade around the packed local football stadiums. The reaction from the fans was overwhelming and showed how strong the link is between the two sports. On the whole, supporters of Birmingham City, Aston Villa and Coventry City are not united by much, but in terms of joining in the support of their local cricket team, they were as one. The day we were paraded at Villa Park was especially memorable because it was before a Cup game and their goalkeeper, Mark Bosnich, with whom I shared several mutual friends, saved a penalty to reassert the impression that he was a superb player when the pressure was on. It was when the game was of less importance that Mark's concentration could slide. Sounds familiar, doesn't it?

Yet the most memorable feature of all came a few months after the season had finished when I had a benefit function at Lord's cricket ground; a real honour in itself. To cap it all off, however, George Best was the speaker. George was brilliant, but he came with a reputation ten times worse than Brian Lara for punctuality. With a couple of minutes to go before he was meant to be speaking there was no sign of him and someone said, "I told you he wouldn't turn up." But with search parties about to be sent out, in he came, joining World Cup winner Gordon Banks, who was my other guest. We sat together for three hours - a fascinating time - during which time George drank three bottles of wine, some soda and ate a few vegetables. He talked of the reasons he went to America - to escape the intrusions of privacy in part - about adventures he had experienced and shared some views on women. They say if you've been an athlete you have a better chance of living a fast life for longer. Best was 49 and looked a million dollars on the night, he was testimony to that, though his fast living eventually caught up with him.

At the end of the dinner I accompanied him home to Chelsea. We pitted several times for a series of "one last drink" stops and didn't make it back to George's place until dawn. It was an amazing night. It wasn't hard to see why he had a drink problem, either. People thrust glasses into

PARADING TROPHIES AT VILLA PARK

At the end of our ground-breaking season, we were invited to show off our three trophies on a victory lap of local football stadiums during half-time in games. This day, at a packed Villa Park, the atmosphere was electric. Check out my facial expression, though (extreme right). I was wasted. I've a whole lot of Ecstasy in me here and that, combined with the buzz of walking out in front of more than 30,000 people, was pretty intense. This was pretty much the image I'd have been seeing through my own eyes - the haziness of this picture would have been my focus. I've seen musicians take the stage in similar states. I've also seen them make fools of themselves at times by doing so. They end up forgetting the lyrics or chords. Steven Tyler, the Aerosmith singer, once told me about the occasion the band had changed their set list around so that what was traditionally the last song of the set became the opener. Tyler was so out of it he sang the opening song and left the stage thinking the gig was over! He also said that in earlier days that he'd believed that "anything worth doing was worth overdoing", but that it was an attitude that nearly killed him. I knew what he meant. I discovered more about 'fame' the day after another Aerosmith gig I attended. I was surprised to read my own name in a review. Much of the journalist's copy was about me being in attendance. It made comparisons in looks between me and the band's front man - the clothes we wore etc. The fact I was in a back stage area was even mentioned. I'd only gone to watch the band - anonymously I thought.

his hand all night and nobody would let us buy a thing. I left Lord's with £12,000 in my pocket and didn't spend a penny of it; one of the major perks of being a professional sportsman.

A couple of years later I bumped into George in Birmingham's China Town. He was walking down the street late one evening but, within a few minutes, we had embarked on an impromptu night of revelry. It was a killer night. He took me to several places I never knew existed - despite the fact that I had been based in the city for 16 years - proving correct the saying that age and experience means more than youth and desire. George never played in an FA Cup final - surprising, really - but spent most of his life celebrating as if he had just won it. I didn't detect any regrets. I think he enjoyed himself plenty just the way his life was.

Best lived his life in the spotlight, and so did we, although mostly it was trained on Brian Lara. In amongst all the demands of the treble season, Lara and I flew to South Africa to play some floodlit games for a Rest of the World XI in aid of team-mate Allan Donald's benefit season. During the flight to Johannesburg Lara slept. Whilst he was doing so I observed a TV crew accompanying us on the trip filming the world's greatest batsman. The guy's camera was close up. It was the epitome of intrusion.

At the end of the treble season, with all its tense games and extended celebrations, I was exhausted. I think we all were. The effort that goes into such seasons is outrageous. The physical and mental exertion is, I believe, probably the same as a lesser team would put in over two and a half seasons. There were so many big games; so many crucial moments; so many times when we had to find that extra ounce of energy and inspiration to make the difference. It was exhausting. The euphoria, however, was like a drug. Think of the warm feeling people talk of when their first drink starts to kick in. It's like that, only much better.

It's hard to replace those feelings. The massive high I felt when a part of the action became addictive and I couldn't easily replace the excitement of competing in a game that could go either way. It also became harder to wind down after games. One big problem was wherever you went people spoke about cricket. It was really great that people embraced the team's successes - however - a salesmen wouldn't appreciate a grilling about his work every time he went for a bite to eat or a drink. Sometimes it made you want to be elsewhere.

Over previous summers I had been given greater responsibility by the team leader and coach. Their confidence in me rubbed off to great effect and I had learnt to control match situations; I knew I had enough tricks in my game to keep anyone guessing. I feared nobody. Any fear of failure or worry that I would be bollocked by the coach after the game disappeared. I knew my game plan - often a big bag of bluffs by now - and had the balls to try almost anything.

Our successes began to attract more attention. A new audience appeared and mingled with familiar people I'd spent many hours with in the past. On-pitch euphoria stopped disappearing once the day's adrenalin faded. I had always been able to relax and wind down through beer or good food. Now things started to change.

I knew I had to be careful. In the past I had always had the sense to walk away from real trouble, to spot the people who might lead me astray. Now, however, those people were the ones offering me the best off-pitch experiences.

Within 12 months I was recreating the buzz of that success through drugs. Perhaps it was simply due to exhaustion, but everything I had wanted to achieve since I had been a kid started to mean less and less once I'd actually achieved it.

People have asked why I didn't go in to rehab then. Why didn't I just ask for help? The truth is that I didn't dare talk it through with anyone. I feared I would simply be fired. That's still the case. As the years pass it has become clear that I was not the only one in the side experiencing the same problems. Three of us have now gone public, and one or two others may have decided to keep quiet. I knew that at the time, but didn't say anything. For one reason or another, the experiences of that era took their toll on several of us. We couldn't cope with the success, the attention or the workload. I suppose you could say the success went to our heads. We needed help. We needed off field support. We needed additional people to be a barrier between us and possible problems. Unfortunately there was no help available. At that time the club didn't even have a press officer.

The team had secured three trophies and lost the final of the only other competition. Even that was largely due to the toss of a coin as Worcestershire enjoyed much the better of the conditions in the NatWest final. It was always desperately difficult having to bat first in those September finals as the dew handed the seamers a massive advantage. On that occasion it was worse still, with rain meaning the game went into a second day. We had to bat on both mornings! During Worcestershire's innings, Tom Moody, a mate, hit me for a monumental six - I'd personally get a bus if I had to walk the distance the Australian struck my best effort.

Sitting in the changing rooms at Lord's after defeat, I had a sense that it could only be the start of a long descent. In a way I wish the story could stop there. It would be much neater, but life isn't like that. So often a happy ending is just a story that finishes too soon. After all, if you've climbed the highest mountain, to go any further you have to come back down. And from the glory of a happy changing room at Lord's, there was only one way to travel.

We were joined by members of the club's committee who shook our hands and thanked us for our efforts. It was a nice touch. No doubt their good humour was helped by the fact they had won around £150,000 by placing a bet on us at the start of the season!

It had become apparent that Woolmer was going to take the job of coach of South Africa. He had been superb and his departure would be noticed. The morning after we'd completed our treble at Bristol, I was with Woolmer in the reception of our hotel when the call came through from Dr Ali Bacher, the South African supremo. Woolmer had it transferred to his room. That was the time reality struck home. Ali had also made a surprise appearance the night before our B&H final two months earlier. I spoke with my ex-boss in our hotel bar, mostly about our time in Johannesburg with me let loose. He knew I'd learn a lot on the pitch - and off it. He was hugely impressed with what we'd transformed ourselves into. It's ironic that the cricket we played when Warwickshire cleaned up was the exact style of play I experienced weekly when I was 18 with Bacher as my boss. He's a man who gets results. Woolmer was his target.

Bob had arrived at Edgbaston as coach in March 1991. The previous coach, Bob Cottam, and the captain, Andy Lloyd, had clashed publicly over that winter. Cottam felt our skipper wasn't always worthy of selection. The discrepancy led to Warwickshire being minus a coach. Within six weeks the club's chairman, Bob Evans, had also gone. An emergency committee meeting was called when Evans was away in Bournemouth and he was voted out. At one stage he had suggested that all interests be declared by those on the committee; some obviously thought it a barbed request. Shame; I always reckoned he was a fine man with the best interests of the club at heart.

So it was a turbulent atmosphere that greeted Woolly when he walked into Edgbaston three months later. Everyone expected South African Clive Rice to be given the coach's job. Yet Woolly's friendship with Dennis Amiss, forged through their mutual experiences in Kerry Packer's World Series, Test and South African rebel cricket, proved telling.

The thing that immediately stood out with Woolly was the time he would spend trying to get his point across. We would debate anything and everything, talking cricket for hours in an attempt to understand what could turn our fortunes. It was time well spent; the four years he spent with us at Edgbaston took the club to a different level. He was superb. A father figure; keen as they come and with a professional approach and attention to detail that was allied to excellent communication skills and a healthy portion of common sense.

One of the first things Woolmer did was insist that a physiotherapist travelled everywhere with the team. In retrospect it seems hard to believe that this wasn't always the case, but before Bob arrived we had been forced to rely on the opponent's physio being honest when treating and advising us. All this whilst he and their team knew the state of play; it led to many occasions when we were told that a bowler would "be better to sit this one out" while an opponent's batsmen made merry. The alterations made by Bob finally made the term "professional cricketer" an appropriate label for Warwickshire cricketers.

He wasn't afraid to be different. He judged Allan Donald's rhythm by listening to the noise the bowler made as he ran up, his feet on the floor and the sound as he passed the umpire. He did this with his back to AD. Over time he fine-tuned Donald's approach to the crease and played a significant part in his development into the world's premier fast bowler. Every delivery AD bowled was like an unwanted alarm call to our opposition. Such was the fear his pace instilled in our opponents that I remember a non-striker coming down the wicket and simply saying to the new, incoming batsman, "We're all doomed."

Bob's attention to detail was fastidious. He embraced new ideas as few men of his age tend to do and was open to any suggestion. He gave us the confidence to try new things and helped us understand what we were doing. The issue of reverse swing was a classic example and, under him, we learnt that chewing Extra Strong Mints helped the ball swing more. We even worked out that the spices in curry lingering in our saliva helped with shining.

Bob also used his experience as a pretty good hockey player. He often talked about batting with hockey tech-niques, specifically trying to hit the ball when it was directly underneath the eyes, and one day ended up playing a charity game with us just to demonstrate what he was talking about. Trying to make a point in the car on the way to the ground he finally said, "I'll bloody well have to show you what I mean." Besides, his wife and children were in Cape Town at the time and we knew he would be pining for them. The game took place on the Britannic Assurance pitch, just up the road from Edgbaston, and I was at the other end when he came to the crease. I can only say that he really did bat like God that day. I've no doubt that he still had the ability to play professionally at this stage - even though he was in his mid-40s - but his fitness would simply not have allowed it. He smashed it to all parts; it was made more impressive by his repeatedly predicting the outcome of the next delivery he'd face. I'd only seen Lara and Sobers do that. Bob showed that if you worked hard, thought positively and backed yourself, anything was possible.

He put the smiles back on faces at Edgbaston, creating an environment where everyone wanted to be involved. The hard work didn't seem that hard. He actually passed on the ability to self-coach if and when things were going against you. He taught us how to asses and correct things within games and taught us about the importance of imagination and affirmation. He was miles ahead of other coaches at that time.

He was always hugely suspicious about what we were up to off the pitch, however. It became an endless source of fun. In Trinidad on his first pre-season tour with us, he announced at 10pm that our accommodation front door key would be left above the entrance door frame at all times. He then moved into the room next to the front door. Eight hours later I returned with a team-mate to find Woolly hadn't kept his promise, he'd retained the key. Our knocking brought a rapidly learning coach to our aid; the excuse that we had gone for a walk to ease our jet-lagged legs didn't totally convince him.

Next year we went to Cape Town. When Bob started worrying that our social life was detracting from our training sessions, he had us relocated to a health spa in the wilderness. Very soon that led to players creeping out in the night and returning to Cape Town.

On one such trip I returned at dawn to find a large, white object crouched down in bushes by the complex entrance. It was Woolmer. He had risen early to catch us as we came in. I crept in around the back and went to bed only to be confronted by an irate coach who asked where I had been and how much sleep I'd had. I denied everything and my tour continued, but what the incident showed was

A RECORD RUN CHASE

Setting a record by chasing down 322 to win at Lord's to win the Nat West in 1993. I felt we could win even at the halfway stage when it might have appeared to some that Sussex were home and dry. I remember walking out to bat with the score at 18 for two. The Long Room was almost silent, with only the occasional, almost embarrassed hand clap. I knew we could win. I made 60 - described by the media as a "violent" innings - before being given out caught behind after missing the ball by several inches. It didn't matter. Asif Din - another guy who often pro-duced his best when it mattered most - and Dermot took us to victory.
People look at the scoreboard and think it was a perfect batting pitch. Actually it was far from it. Sussex reckoned they should play their shots because, sooner rather than later, an unplayable ball would come along. They batted very well and we bowled poorly. But we went at them hard and they soon became rattled. Had we not won it seems that our coach, Woolmer, would have been fired. We won five more trophies within the next 24 months.

how much he cared. He lived every ball of every game and took great pride in our success.

Bob demanded maximum effort at all times. He gave 100% himself and expected it of all the players. He was forever drumming into us the importance of plenty of sleep and avoiding alcohol, but he knew there had to be times to unwind and have a laugh. I loved working with him. I learned a great deal.

Deep down I'd like to think Bob understood that all players are different. I remember a story I was told by former Australian leg-spinner Kerry O'Keefe. He and team-mate Doug Walters had shared a hotel room during a Test Match in New Zealand. The preparation for their performances had been contrasting. O'Keefe had gone to bed early evening, Walters not so. Nearer 6am in fact, when he had collapsed in a heap on top of his room-mate.

Breakfast had been contrasting again, O'Keefe drank orange juice and had cereals; Walters had to be plied with coffee and cigarettes. Walters scored a mammoth 247 without being dismissed. O'Keefe himself was dismissed first ball. Later in the day Walters was a national hero. I could provide hundreds of other examples Colin 'Olli' Milburn was the same. I knew Milburn from when I was a kid as our parents knew each other. On the 1968 England tour to the Caribbean Olli was warned about his alcohol consumption. A senior figure told him: "You don't always have to have a pint, Colin." Legend has it that Milburn went straight to the bar and said: "Two halves of beer, please."

Incidentally, I recall Olli Milburn once acting as Man Of The Match adjudicator in a game we played against Scotland in the 1987 Benson & Hedges Cup. By then he was weighing in at around 18 stone and spent most of the day enjoying himself in a corporate hospitality marquee rather than watching the game. He surfaced at the end, had a quick look at the scorecard and gave the match award to Andy Moles as he was "the only one with a waist-line that resembles mine."

Bob couldn't always coax the best from such charac-ters. When he returned to Warwickshire as coach in 2000, the club signed fast bowler Ed Giddins, who, despite a very good start, eventually fell out with Bob. Personally I thought Ed was a damn good player and a good guy, too. But he sure was different. They'd have been on a different planet sometimes. And Bob couldn't always appreciate that being different was ok. He made an early mistake by referring to Giddins as 'Simon', but the bowler took 84 first-class wickets in his first season and still finished with 150 victims at 24 apiece for the club. He could bowl, but a breakdown in communication meant that his relationship with the club soured. That was a shame because Ed was actually a very dedicated sportsman. It's just he also wanted more from life and Bob couldn't always empathise.

Our success with Bob so nearly never happened. Both he and Asif Din were within a hair's breadth of being released from the club at the end of the 1993 season, only for us to win the last final of the year in the NatWest Trophy, and save both their careers. Asif just battled away and scored a match-winning hundred at Lord's, which led not only to a new deal with the club, but to a benefit season and, eventually, a place on the club's committee. Bob, meanwhile, not only stayed at the club to oversee our treble in the next season, but also went on to win the South African coaching job. Without our win at Lord's in 1993, I'm sure that wouldn't have happened.

There were times we made fun of Bob. On his first pre-season tour in Trinidad we stopped the team bus at a KFC. Bob, having said he didn't like that sort of food, then took it upon himself to order for the whole team. Or so we thought. Actually, the mountain of dead chicken that he hauled back on to the bus was just for him. Bob liked his food to come by the bucketload. He was a man with a large appetite for life.

Another time he accused me of placing a large traffic cone on top of his brand new car. It wasn't me; it was the team's vice-captain, Tim Munton. In the end I suggested Bob ask to view the hotel's CCTV footage, but he was reluctant as it might just show up the tray of sandwiches he'd had delivered to his room an hour after dinner. Munton eventually owned up and I ordered two breakfasts to be delivered to Woolmer's room in the morning as punishment. I bet he ate them both.

Bob believed I was lazy in my approach to preparation and training. It wasn't that I was lazy - quite the opposite in fact - I just had the energy to both work and play hard.

We certainly had a lot of fun on those pre-season tours. Another time, along with several other members of the Warwickshire team, I was invited for drinks on board The Royal Yacht Britannia by members of the crew. It was a revealing night, with lurid tales of excess on the luxurious yacht enough to make our ears stand on end. If those walls could talk...

Allan Donald and Shaun Pollock later told me that Bob had regularly told them that I was, along with Pat Symcox, the hardest cricketer he had ever worked with. We drove him nuts. He couldn't understand my view that if you missed the fun in life, you missed the boat. I believed the Katherine Hepburn line, "If you obey all the rules, you miss all the fun." Opportunity doesn't always come knocking twice. I wanted to suck the marrow from every day and he wanted me to preserve myself for tomorrow.

I know I frustrated him, but I also won him games. Both Pat and I would scrap like hell when the pressure was on. He persevered with us both because he knew we were worth it.

Woolly's murder in Jamaica during the World Cup in March 2007 left a scar. Many members of the Warwickshire sides of the mid-90s spoke to each other in the following days; shock was the shared emotion. In amongst that, however, was a sense that we were all incredibly fortunate to have been able to work alongside him and to have seen incredible amounts of success along the way.

I was taking a Prince's Trust session at Edgbaston on the day it was announced that his death was the result of murder. Despite the sense of grief and outrage, his positive influence shone through. I ran the session exactly as I'd seen him run them. The emphasis was on fun, little challenges were set and everyone was involved.

The kids had a great time, but it brought back memories. Fond but painful memories. When I'd been with Bob in Cape Town we would sometimes run sessions together. Other Warwickshire players did the same. We saw how he worked, how he thought and how he communicated. It was a tremendously valuable experience and one I'd damn glad to have had. His methods will live on.

As far as I'm concerned, any accusations directed at Bob Woolmer regarding match-fixing are a complete load of garbage. He was steeped in the spirit of cricket from the time, as a baby, his father put a small bat and ball into his cot and wished that it would be his life.

Bob would never have done anything that damaged the game he loved. He may have found it hard to say "no" to Thai food, but he wasn't greedy when it came to money; quite the opposite, in fact. Very few top coaches would have been prepared to live in the basic one-bedroom flat in the National Stadium in Pakistan that Bob made his home for so long. It's interesting that nobody who knew Bob well thinks he was involved. Sure, a few journalists who hardly knew him made a link because of his relationship with the disgraced Hansie Cronje. It's a shame that the laws in this country mean that once someone dies it can be open season on them. The dead can't sue for libel.

I was personally never approached to throw a game. Not in England, not in Hong Kong, South Africa, Singapore or Australia. There were rumours, however; although not when Woolly was our coach. Warwickshire had to win a game against Notts in the 1980 Sunday League to secure the trophy. The game was played at the mid-point of a championship game that Notts had to win and rumour had it that Clive Rice and Richard Hadlee were left out of their side which lost the vital one-dayer to encourage us to bat poorly on Monday, the final day of the championship fixture. Maybe, but it would be an equally reasonable assumption to conclude that Rice and Hadlee were rested on Sunday to make sure they were fully fit for bowling on Monday.

Frankly I believe that Bob was killed precisely because he was so clean; so determined not to allow any of that seedy world to enter the sport he loved. He was certainly no match-fixer.

At the time of the murder in the Caribbean I know that Bob was in the process of starting an academy in Cape Town. He won't be around to see it, but I believe every-thing he planned should still go ahead and his family's announcement of a trust fund to ensure his work endures hopefully will see that happen. He had done so much work in the area - much of it for free - and it would have delighted him to think that future generations of kids could have the chance to play the game that he loved so dearly. I'd go and work in it, if only in his honour. But it will also require funding. A couple of big charity games featuring world stars to raise funds would guarantee its longevity.

Eventually I do think he gave up on me and I can't say I really blame him. The straw that broke the camel's back was a pre-season tour to South Africa. More specifically, it was the flight to Cape Town.

Within a few days of our treble season finishing many of the team had dispersed across the globe and left us feel-ing that we had not had ample opportunity to celebrate together. The pre-season tour to Cape Town the following year seemed an ideal time. To me, anyway. Confidence was high. Everyone was pleased to be back in each other's company once more.

After travelling down to Heathrow, we checked in and visited the duty free shops and bars. After an hour or so we were called through to board for the ten-and-a-half hour flight to South Africa's most picturesque city. As soon as I entered the plane I recognised a stewardess who had been working on previous flights we had taken as a team. She'd altered her schedule to be on our flight after finding out that the team were due to fly to Cape Town. Several of us had spent a bit of time in her company on a previous trip to Harare.

About an hour into the flight, I was invited into the cockpit of the plane to chat with those in charge. It was explained how everything worked and, after about ten minutes, I returned to my seat, stopping briefly on the way to make arrangements with the stewardess to meet up over the next couple of weeks.

A little while later I checked my wallet for cash as I made my way to the toilets. After closing the door I was shocked to find a small quantity of cocaine and an ecstasy tablet squeezed in between some credit cards. Considering I had just checked through one of the worlds biggest airports it was a moment that completely took my breath away.

I flushed the cocaine away. I had never been a big fan of this drug and I could pretty much always take or leave it. In truth, I consider it to be a woman's drug, though I know a stack of men take it. The ecstasy tablet was much more of a temptation. If I had an addiction to anything by this stage it was pills. I took it; if nothing else, I reasoned, it would help make for an interesting flight. More interesting than I intended.

I returned to my seat feeling hollow, by now I knew I was a shadow of myself. By now nothing really mattered. I abandoned myself to fate. Sitting next to me were two players and a keen supporter who came out to follow the side for the duration of the tour. Luckily for me, because of a lack of leg room, I was sat on the edge of the row of seats by the aisle.

My position gave me a clear view of a girl sat just the other side of the walkway. She was pretty. I arrogantly asked my colleagues how long it would take me to engage positively with her; they must have thought my confidence was borne of the pre-flight drinking. Anyway, their replies varied from no chance to 20 minutes.

Leaning across the aisle I caught the girl's eye. She removed her walkman headphones: "Are you walking to the top of the aisle?" she asked with a twinkle. I didn't need further invitation, so off we went. My team-mates were open-mouthed; so was I if truth be known, but what was I going to do?

After entering the tiny plane toilet all hell broke loose. Fantastic. We were in there for some time. Suddenly there was a bang at the door; I ignored it, thinking that it was some team-mates having a laugh. A minute or so later there was a second thud on the folding door, followed by the sound of some commotion outside. There is only one way out of an aeroplane toilet and it struck me that whoever was standing outside must have clocked exactly what was going on. There was no point in worrying at that stage, however. We carried on.

Suddenly a mighty crash brought the door down on my left shoulder. There were seven faces peering in at us. I gave a boyish smile; didn't know what else to do. It was obviously the wrong response. It later transpired the person who had kicked down the door was the stewardess who had changed flights to catch up in Cape Town.

All eyes were on us as we rearranged ourselves and made the long walk down the aisle to our seats. We received a mixed reaction from our fellow passengers. The young ones gave us the thumbs up; the older ones frowned. You can probably imagine the conversation from my team-mates when I finally sat down.

Suddenly Woolmer appeared. Clearly angry, but not sure which issue to attack me on. The coach asked me, "Were you wearing your club blazer when the doors were opened?" It was the last question I expected and seemed such a bizarre detail. I laughed, not out of disrespect, more because of the absurdity of the whole situation. I believe that was the moment he washed his hands of me and that I'd become a lost cause.

Despite regular off-field lapses, our friendship continued whenever we met up. I believe Bob's spell at Edgbaston was a great time of learning for everyone. What we did on the pitch was filled with fun and laughter; this is what we remember.

Many hours later we touched down in South Africa and had to disembark. In doing so we had to walk past the cabin crew, not the most comfortable of walks. But everyone still in possession of a sense of humour laughed when the girl ran through the airport at Cape Town into the arms of her boyfriend.

I'm not proud of anything that took place on that plane. It is worth saying, however, that nobody was hurt or threatened. My marriage was over and I certainly wasn't asking for the doors to be kicked open. Besides, I've seen worse things happen in public - far worse.

The reason it happened? I'd stopped caring about the consequences. Nothing mattered.

No Direction Home

OVER THE YEARS CRICKET has taken me to some amazing places around the world. It has led to me spending time with many people in the public eye; people known for vastly different careers.

The experiences I gained in South Africa changed my life. From my first exposure of working in townships under Dr. Ali Bacher and playing there, my time in the country taught me much that I was later to use in the coaching and mentoring programmes that became my focus as I rebuilt my life.

I'll always be grateful for the part Bob Woolmer played in my education as a person. Bob played Test cricket as an all-rounder for England and became Warwickshire coach in 1991. He then coached the South African Test side once they had been received back into the sporting fold and, of course, subsequently, Pakistan's national team. Bob helped me represent St Augustine's, a well-known cricket club in South Africa and a place best known as former England and Worcestershire star Basil D`Oliveira`s spiritual home.

I was the first professional at Basil's club. That meant a lot. I knew his son Damian, who I played against when we'd taken on Worcestershire in a Lord's final and I knew the family quite well. Basil D`Oliveira`s exploits at St Augustine's were legendary; I looked through old score-books and he had scored centuries so often it was scarcely believable.

Being the first white guy to take the field for the Cape Coloured team meant even more.

The community within Saints had a passion for life despite terrible hardships Apartheid forced on them. The whole community were marched out of their home area, called District Six, during the late 1960s under military escort. They had to watch as their homes were bulldozed and were then rounded up and taken to the Cape Flats; a disused sandy wasteland out of view the 'other' side of Table Mountain. They started from scratch. Remarkably, out of the chaos rose a stronger people. They looked after one another and developed a new resilience, pride and incredible ability to forgive. But don't mess with these people. They learned to fight back. A recent statistic I read said that there are now thought to be over 10 million guns housed in these same Cape Flats.

There was an element of the American 'deep south' about South Africa. Everything depended on skin tone. It was hard for me to come to terms with a country where the laws were based around the colour of your skin. It made no sense logically or morally. It was, fortunately, bound to fail. Eventually. There was to be a hell of a lot of suffering before that happened, however, and echoes of the problem will live on for a century or more. Some days I would go to the beach with a girl who'd be hell bent on gaining the best tan possible, sometimes she'd talk of "blacks or coloureds" in a negative way. When I asked her why she wanted to attain their colour she couldn't answer.

I spent much time around my team-mates. We may have had very different hair, but we all knew how to let it down. They enjoyed life and I enjoyed their company.

Many times I was very grateful for it, too. One night we entered a bar only to be met by two men with shotguns. They checked us for weapons then stamped our hands. I glanced at the words printed on to my hand: 'Farewell' it said. There were only three whites in the area among many thousands and not everyone welcomed us; fair enough, really. You can't blame them for their distrust. The captain of my side told me not to worry. He said I'd be fine because of who I was sitting with.

There were dangers, however. People presumed, because I was white, that I had money and there were a few incidents when my car was literally covered by people trying to get in through the boot, all the doors and the sun roof. Only after they recognised someone in the car did they stop.

My Warwickshire team-mate, Andy Moles, once had to lie flat across the seats of his car to avoid being shot in the aftermath of a bank robbery and there was a realisation that if you found yourself in the wrong place at the wrong time, there wasn't very much you could do. South Africa was tough and territorial. One of my team-mates kept a Luger hand gun by his car handbreak to deal with such problems. In that respect there's little difference between parts of South Africa and Compton, South Central or any other poor part of Los Angeles.

All these incidents occurred only a few months after the Apartheid laws changed. For the first time in many years, people of all ethnicities were mixing with one another, in the same bars, restaurants and buses, all on equal terms. Tensions were inevitable.

On the field there were also problems with plenty of terse comments which took the usual on-field sledging to a totally different level. Being white and being the club professional put extra responsibility on my shoulders; later in my career I think this added responsibility helped me deal with many on field pressure situations.

At a game in Mitchell's Plaine - a black and coloured area - things certainly did heat up. The game was going down to the wire and I had the responsibility of winning it for our side. One of their batsmen shouted that he was "going to smack my white backside", but my next delivery smacked him straight above his left eye. Off he went to hospital. We needed one more wicket for victory but the new batsman was the retired batsman's brother. As he came onto the square he was abusing me and threatening all sorts. Finally he took strike and, after facing one delivery, ran up the wicket to whack me with his bat, shouting "son of a whore".

There was a reason he was batting at 11, however. Instead of hitting me, he tripped over my feet and took a crashing blow in the middle of the pitch. Meanwhile, one of our fielders threw the ball over the top of the stumps and the bails were removed. He was out and the game was over. To add insult to his injuries, the number 11 was given out by an umpire, who happened to be the only other white guy in the vicinity. The two brothers took a little while to placate, but within an hour the healing power of a couple of beers had done the trick. We were all getting along just fine.

Later that summer St Augustine's were to break new ground by playing their first game at Newlands, Cape Town's Test cricket ground. The country's laws had prevented my team-mates from playing at the venue in the past. As if to underline the significance of the day, an earth tremor marked the occasion. I scored my only century of the season during that game amidst being repeatedly called a "black lover" by my white opponents.

Still, the ability to work in such places; to go amongst those who were dispossessed and untrusting of whites, was invaluable. Those lessons armed me for my work today.

Perhaps surprisingly, America is a place where my cricket career and Warwickshire's record trophy-winning achievements have been best rewarded with acclaim, acknowledgement and the ability to 'open doors'.

Cricket and the United States are not seen to go hand in hand. Their showing in the 2004 ICC Champions Trophy did little to dispel the myth that this country favours baseball, basketball and American football and will never compete against other countries with an ingrained cricketing history.

Clayton Lambert, a destructive batsman who played for the West Indies before moving to the States and representing that country, put it best. "Sometimes people think it's like polo, played on horseback," he said. "And I remember one guy thought it was a game involving insects!"

However, people should check out the facts. The earliest record of the game being played in the U.S. dates back to April 1709 in Virginia. George Washington's troops are also known to have played cricket almost 70 years later at Valley Forge in 1778. Games used to attract thousands of spectators. Figures show that around four million American residences tune in to watch cricket on satellite, while a surprisingly large number of people in the country - many of them ex-pats - also follow the game via cricket websites such as CricInfo.

I had always seen America as the land of opportunity. Anything was possible there. It is a huge country, with a huge audience and market. There is a massive disparity between rich and poor and, perhaps most importantly, the people are more open to invention. There was a huge amount of scope for my scheme.

The first contact I had with Ted Hayes was in 2001. He was manager of a tour of Britain by a Los Angeles cricket team called Homies and the POPz, sponsored by Maxim magazine. He'd led two previous UK tours by what was styled as 'this most unusual of all cricket teams'. Their stated aim was to revolutionise the way the world sees cricket - and they'd certainly made an impact. In fact they'd created such a stir that the Walt Disney corporation had already picked up the film rights to their incredible story, while two full-length television documentaries had been made and they'd featured on the BBC, Sky TV and even the Oprah Winfrey show.

I was running a Cricket Without Boundaries session in the Edgbaston indoor school and within minutes of the team's arrival in the practice area I was struck by their enthusiasm for the game. Their vocal encouragement for each other was infectious. I hadn't witnessed such spirit in the sport since I was a kid. It reminded me of everything that had first attracted me to the game and was a breath of fresh air. At that very moment I decided to see what I could do for this group. My work and experiences over the previous few years was too closely linked to let this chance meeting pass. It was a matter of putting things together.

Ted ran Dome Village in L.A. alongside two colleagues Katy Haber and Ronda Flanzbaum. The village, a series of fibreglass igloos designed to give protection to some of the many homeless people in the city, was located on an old disused car park on the inappropriately titled Golden Avenue in downtown Los Angeles. It wouldn't ever have existed but for this black Rastafarian. Outside its perimeter fence often was a half kilometre line of people living under cardboard; the recently homeless will have had tents. All awaited a vacancy inside. They needed food, showers and understanding.

Most importantly, these people wanted safety. They needed to be far away from the grasp of the pimps and drug dealers that rule these streets. It's a sorry sight. Here you can get killed for catching the wrong person's eye. It's a place where you can feel desperation in the air.

During this period I lived with Katy Haber in West Hollywood. Every night she'd give me a different tour of everything L.A offers you if you're seasoned and know what's happening. This trip took in the best restaurants, beaches, bars, hillside residences and nightlife.

Every time the apartment phone rang there'd be a name from the movie world talking on the other end. Katy'd had a long relationship with Sam Peckinpah - a guy renowned as one of the last great American film directors - who had been responsible for classics sich as *The Wild Bunch* and *Straw Dogs*. Haber in her own right has been involved in many big movies. Peckinpah had taken on, and completely removed the chains and shackles of Hollywood, altering the rules on what was acceptable. The battle lasted over a decade. People I met said that Sam Peckinpah was many things - genius, brilliant, pioneer, maverick, difficult, stubborn, a lunatic, madman, alcoholic, and drug addict. Most had been said of me. I felt as if I knew the guy.

One day Ted Hayes drove me to Marvin Gaye's house in Crenshaw. Ted had stayed there with the Motown legend for long periods, residing in the rear garden house. Gaye had appreciated and supported the issues and injustices which Ted brought to the surface.

Standing in the same spot where Marvin Gaye was shot dead was unnerving. It felt like time hadn't moved on, there was still an atmosphere. People who knew Gaye described a troubled soul. Ted said too many outside distractions had got to the singer. It proved money doesn't buy happiness; just a bigger playground.

In the UK, if you give your kids some dinner money, you may be worried they spend it on unhealthy food, or, at worst, 10 cigarettes. In the U.S., there are people making a living selling drugs to kids for as little as $2. Temptation is everywhere and the perceived glamour of the gang lifestyle seduces many into making the wrong choices. In a society where so many feel there aren't opportunities for them, it's hardly surprising that people fall victim to such temptation. To some extent I can understand their desire to escape their reality, if only for a short time. I'd done the same thing myself. It only makes things worse in the long term, but when you're a kid you don't always appreciate that.

Ted's daughter, Joanna Hayes, won a gold medal in the 100m hurdles at the 2004 Athens Olympics; he doesn't mention it but her many achievements mean a lot. She was the only American to win a solo gold; all the others were in team events. Joanna predicted the exact time she'd run, 12.37, and then went out and achieved it - a rarity in life. It was a new Olympic record for the event.

The village Ted fronted was a godsend for those whose lives had hit rock bottom. The igloos safely housed families when the streets had been their only other option. It's not glamorous, but more than a few of those who spent time there owe their change of circumstances to its existence. All the inhabitants would have experienced life without shelter; most have some experience of the evil world of pimps, pushers and hookers. So often there people's experience of the police amounts to little more than being moved on more times than they remember.

Many times in this city I've been reminded of how homelessness doesn't respect reputations. In the city of Los Angeles reside 27,000 homeless Vietnam War veterans. Over L.A. County itself the total hovers at around 85,000 people sleeping without shelter every night of the year. The reason for street living varies; many run from violence and unhappiness, often stemming from what should have been family homes. Some can't cope with their pasts and some just don't have the skills to build a future. Nearly all of them are damaged. Mental illness goes with the territory. This is a place where you need to concentrate on the present. The future is a luxury few can afford to think about.

Meeting some of the people that lived within Dome Village proved an education. 'Ed' had become homeless through no fault of his own. The fact that he had served three terms as a bomb diffuser in Vietnam didn't buy him any favours. It didn't mean anything. His job, when employed within the U.S. military, was to work alone up front defusing Vietnamese booby traps, whilst his many reliant colleagues followed. A brilliant brain, a trooper technician now thankful for the fibreglass roof over his head.

One day Katy and I spent time with an elderly lady called Patty who was living on the streets; her lifetime's belongings in a supermarket trolley. They have big trolleys in L.A.. She showed us photos taken thirty years before, this woman had been a regular dancing double in Hollywood movies, she'd worked the biggest ocean liners and Vegas had been a place where regular requests for her talents saw lucrative financial windfalls. She had been beautiful; a few years homelessness had stolen that beauty. She turned out to be in her 50s, she wasn't old at all.

There is a sinister cocaine, freebase, chystal meth and heroin trafficking network in L.A.. The hard drug trade doesn't offer profit for the poor because the market gets taken over by professionals who don't spread their profits around freely.

In South Central, one homeless guy said, "The heat only makes the rats bigger here dude." This is in a place where pimps hire out their "Hooker Hoes" for $10 if he needs it. All this to create a "Strawberry fund" from which that pimp lives in his own style. You don't see too many city council ponds or lakes round these parts. These are indeed Mean Streets.

Late one night we pulled into a garage to fill up the car with fuel. A one-armed petrol attendant came to our aid. Ted shouted to him, "Dude, they're even stealing peoples limbs round here, ain't they?" Much laughter followed. The fact this incident preceded an hour-long drive around the largest homeless blocks of Los Angeles seemed to make it funnier. Here people pass comment but can't control how they are interpreted. Ted had actually lived on these streets, leaving the family home; safe in the knowledge his loved ones would be fine. However, he had some work to do; he needed to be homeless to understand it. It took four years without a roof over his head. He once even starved himself for 37 days for the homeless cause.

Ted is an amazing man; and not at all like you might expect. For a start he is, somewhat surprisingly, a staunch Republican and a strong supporter of George W Bush. Ted believes the worst thing that ever happened to the US. black community was accepting that it needed hand-outs to survive. Indeed, he insists that the Democrats' offers of hand-outs are, on some level, an attempt to maintain the current balance of power. He also points to history, suggesting that black people have fared much less well under Democrats. It was, he says, the party of the slave trade and is now "the Klan party".

Ted is keen to find an area among the black community for the 'new' dome village. That's not due to any sense of apartheid; it is more a sense that he wants the black community to take responsibility for its homeless problem. Around 80% of the inhabitants of the Village were black and he believes that the community must accept the burden of its own problems.

He has strong views on the issue. While he accepts that the black community in America has been disadvantaged, he is adamant that much of the fault lies within. For him, personal responsibility is key, and the sooner that the black community stops blaming other people for their problems and start trying to resolve them the better. There are too many excuses, too many 'inner-city preachers' who blame white racism, and too little action.

"If you want kids to stop shooting people," he has said, "stop blaming white folks for urban tragedy and start blaming the lackadaisical inner-city family culture you support."

Having said that, Ted also believes that the issue of slavery continues to psychologically scar the black community. The fact that these people were once owned and, even in the lifetime of many people, were treated as second-class citizens, has developed a society where many are either bitter or lacking confidence. But, put simply, they must get over that if they are to get on with their lives.

After the devastation and flooding which destroyed New Orleans in 2005, both Bush and Ted stated that the real tragedy that had affected the black community had occurred long, long before Hurricane Katrina. The reasons that so many more black people were killed is that they were living in swamp land where houses should never have been built. Most didn't even have money to get out of town when warnings were broadcast.

The race issue in the U.S. is now inseparable from class and economic issues. The country is divided more on the lines of who is rich and poor than anything, and it just so happens that most of the rich are white and most of the poor are not. It means that racial tensions continue to cause huge problems.

And that's where cricket comes in. Ted believes it encourages personal responsibility and team work. Young people realize that if they screw up, it lets down the whole team. They come to understand that if they are late, or don't show up, it can spoil the day for everyone. Crucially they also come to understand how to cope with their own feelings. That man who questioned if I really meant him to hand a cricket bat, or as he saw it a 3lb wooden weapon, to someone he considered dangerous was missing the point. Playing cricket helps you learn self control; players have to deal with the kind of anger that can be created by being given out incorrectly by an umpire when the ball flicks your pad and not your bat. Far from running down the pitch to threaten that umpire, the former gang members learn to accept those decisions with some kind of grace.

Not everyone who comes along for the Homies & the POPz practices or trials is selected or asked to become involved. Anyone who consistently causes problems or proves to be a disruptive influence is discarded, though Ted is keen to help any individual as much as he can. Some have talent, some don't; the key attribute is enthusiasm and a will to change their lives. If they have those two qualities, they are halfway there.

CRICKET IN THE 'HOOD

No-one would have thought it was possible to change the lives of young people who were apparently dealt the wrong cards at birth by playing cricket. But the virtues that the game teaches kids in the Homies & The Popz team are much stronger than the stiff upper lip and a healthy regard for the rules. And our approach is bearing fruit; in early 2007 Ted managed to secure funding to run a pilot in eight L.A. schools which, if successful, will see the spirit of Cricket Without Boundaries spread across the whole of Los Angeles, helping youngsters like these make something of their lives in a tough, rough world.

Sometimes Ted's passion can get the better of him. His unyielding belief that the spirit of cricket can cure all of society's ills has led to some wonderfully absurd situations. Reasoning that his strategy to build a peace movement had met with some success in California, Ted resolved to broker a lasting peace in Ireland by using the sport to create bonds between the warring factions. He thought that cricket was so powerful that it could actually be used to assist the peace process between Northern Irish Roman Catholics and the Protestant-based British government. Ted calls this strategy for peace "cricket diplomacy".

Anyway, after meeting Gerry Adams and Martin McGuinness, Ted tried to persuade the Sinn Fein leaders to take part in a couple of high-profile games on their next trip to England. Not being knowledgeable of local cultural clashes, Ted did not know that to Northern Irish Roman Catholics, the bat and ball sport was anathema to them. He might as well have tried to persuade them to don Union Jack t-shirts.

Looking back, Ted reasons that sometimes ignorance is bliss. He still insists that if Mr Adams, the symbol of the Northern Irish resistance to British dominance and control, would publicly embrace cricket, which had been a taboo for generations, his efforts would increase the likelihood of peace. It's an interesting thought.

Early 2007 has seen rugby union played at Dublin's Croke Park, home of Gaelic football, and the scene of a dreadful atrocity in 1920 when 13 spectators at a Gaelic game were killed by British forces. That led to the Gaelic Athletic Association banning all 'foreign sports', in other words British administered games such as rugby, football and cricket, from being played on its turf. The Irish national soccer team also played it first home international match at Croke Park. Ted was right in principle; sport can help break down these aged barriers.

We just hope that the concept of Dome Village and the cricket project is an on-going concern. The team and increasing squad is made up of such vulnerable Emergency Housing Program (EHP) people and it does work. But homelessness isn't a trendy issue, particularly in the United States. It's something the majority see sleeping on street pavements, but they don't understand how easily people can fall into it. It's easy, trust me. I hope you never experience it. I did.

The original Dome Village ran into trouble when the landlord hiked up the rent by 700%. Although Ted is confident that he can secure Federal funding to safeguard the future of a new Dome Village, he knows that it will not come cheap. A lot of people are relying on him to provide for them.

The alternatives for homeless people are not attractive. Gang culture is a huge problem in the U.S. and a growing problem in the UK. In England we see playground gangs forming at nine years of age. Unless schemes are provided to encourage people, particularly the young, to channel their energy in a positive direction, it is all too easy to lose them to the criminal underworld.

Prince's Trust students have far more options here in Great Britain whether they're aware of it or not. They often haven't worked out what sort of environment they want to work in. It's not simply a case of getting them to become more studious. For example, some of the issues are drug-related. During a session near Nottingham I spoke to youngsters including several ex-heroin users, we shared experiences and what they had led to. Six months later at Trent Bridge, one of the group approached me outside a discussion and said the talk I'd delivered had helped him get off not just heroin, but also methadone. The guy's life had gone full circle, he could taste food again - little things in such circumstances often make addicts go the full mile to rid themselves of a massive problem.

In America, many people I've worked with of the same age already have a life time's worth of experience within them. In these circumstances it's making sure these people are kept engaged whilst suitable paid work can get them back in the system they've drifted out of, and making everything more law abiding. The same applies here in England, it's just the extremes aren't seen to be as close to the public's front door. One can't be complacent though. Trees grow out of acorns and working in the more extreme places in America puts things into perspective; it allows me to speak from a broader perspective still.

Early trips into America enabled me to make contact with members of gangs, both the "Bloods" and "Crips". An early coaching session saw youngsters undergo compulsory oral and anal spot checks, making sure they had no concealed razor blades!

The Crips were formed in 1971 by Stanley 'Tookie' Williams and Raymond Lee Washington. The pair obviously didn't know what they were creating. Washington was gunned down eight years later, Williams was later described as "America's worst nightmare".

The initial role of the Crips was to protect South Central Los Angeles from other thugs. 30 years later the Crips exist in 42 states through America. Replica Crip gangs have moved continents; South Africa is one such place. Tookie Williams was sentenced to death in 1981 for his part in the murder of four people during robberies in 1979. He spent much of his life on Death Row. For over six years - between 1988 and 1994 - he sat alone in solitary confinement.

In 2004 over 300 Crips died in gang activities in California alone. A gang member will die on average every 30 hours and America's jails are full of victims by association. Time I've spent in areas of L.A. has been colourful, unpredictable, and full of reality checks. One Latino kid shouted, "Every soul has to taste death" as a patrolman cruised past. In Compton you don't wear red or blue, it would make you an immediate target: the colours are gang messages.

Tookie denied the murders. He said he had been set up and there's some evidence he may have been telling the truth. What is not in doubt, however, is that he set up the gang. For that he showed great remorse. He knew he had created a monster and dedicated the remainder of his life to trying to control it. He wrote books warning young people about the dangers of gangs and warning society at large about the lure such groups could have on the dispossessed. We ignore his words at our peril.

Later Arnold Schwarzenegger, in his role as Mayor of California, made the decision to give Tookie the lethal injection. It took 43 minutes to kill him, such was his immense physique.

The Rev Jesse Jackson and singer Joan Baez addressed a large crowd outside San Quentin prison as the Crip leader faded away. The musician Snoop Dog, a former Crips member, and actors Will Smith and Jamie Foxx were also among the protesters. The Crip co-founder was said to be brutal, perhaps it was his way to show others how to act as gang members, but in the latter stages of Williams's life he'd been nominated several times for a Nobel Peace Prize. Archbishop Desmond Tutu, Amnesty International and the Vatican all expressed their regret at his execution. He'll remain a hero to many for various reasons. All kids should read his books but so often it seems that wisdom comes to us when it can no longer do any good.

A few years earlier, on Californian voting day, I walked down Hollywood Boulevard. As I approached a movie house a guy was stood outside with a huge placard. It said, "Don't vote for Arnie, watch his new movie instead." People outside were paying admission fees on a promise of a non-Schwarzenegger vote. Arnie still got in.

I met one Crip member who had known Williams for six years before he'd been incarcerated. 'Chester' told me that Tookie was seen as god-like by this generation. This guy's own experience of gang life - he had been a member of the Crips - was being shot in the face in a bar. The bullet had entered below his left eye socket and exited through his neck.

I asked why he'd become a Crip, he replied he wanted a cooler car and better clothes. Instead gang life had led him to do time in the hardest penitentiaries. Upon release he soon became homeless. This Compton Crip was happy to have survived his experiences. He believed that the decision to give Williams the lethal injection in 2005 was the wrong one; he felt he would have been of far better use giving talks to youngsters within San Quentin penitentiary. One gang member sold 300,000 Tookie Williams badges in the 24 hours leading up to the Crip leader's death - they sold at $5 a time. One can only imagine how this cash was invested.

At this time of life the worst groups of offenders I'd worked with had been in Brinsford Young Offender's unit at Featherstone jail in England. The environment I entered in Los Angeles was to be in a different league. It made the UK seem like a gathering of pussycats.

Walking down Rodeo Drive in Los Angeles we bumped into Death Row Records' CEO Suge Knight. The music industry's hard man was walking with his beautiful young daughter. He weighed in around 330lbs and was dwarfed by two bodyguards. Not only was he supposedly wearing over $2 million worth of bling, Suge was wearing a bulletproof vest as we stood talking. Such protection is a necessity and is worn daily. A few years earlier he'd been driving a car in Las Vegas which was suddenly riddled with bullets and tragically led to Hip-Hop star 2Pac Shukur`s death.

We agreed to meet up later to help us recruit youngsters for our cricket-based activities planned in parks around South Central, Inglewood and the City of Compton. I was delighted as, despite Suge`s image as one of life's more colourful characters, I knew if anyone could help get to a bigger audience then this guy and his contacts could achieve it.

Suge Knight's role within Death Row Records has changed a great deal in recent years. The incarceration term handed out to him for violation of a previous probation had recently seen him do over four years in the infamous Los Angeles County Jail.

Unfortunately we never had the chance to take our conversation further. I was sitting in the White Lotus Club, a venue favoured by Hollywood's livelier characters, when word filtered through that there had been a scuffle in the parking lot. It transpired that Sug and a car valet had been in disagreement. No prizes for guessing who won. The following day he was 'out of town'. His lawyers denied all charges.

One night we sat in a car in Inglewood in downtown L.A. to observe what was going on. It was disturbing. Gang members circled local schools taking every opportunity to recruit new members. We saw more than 30 youngsters stopped by cruising cars. It's hard to say no to gang members; if you're not with them, you're against. And you don't want to be against them. Within a few weeks, three players affiliated with the Homies & the Popz team were dead.

Whenever a cricket practice takes place it does so under the eye of people affiliated with street running. The gang leaders regularly need to replenish their foot soldiers due to deaths, jail sentences and disappearance. Things are blatant, almost unavoidable; those players walking home from practice are too easy to target.

It registered that if I could recreate a Cricket Without Boundaries formula in this sort of district I could make a difference. Although in some ways it appeared craziness to play cricket in these areas, I knew that it could work. The Homies & the POPz would be crucial.

Whether it worked or not would come down to funding. Such money streams exist.

There is so much untapped potential on the streets. People, many of them young, who could make a positive contribution to society if they're given a helping hand. That point was brought home clearly one evening when I went with Ted to collect the comedian Elzie Alexander. On the way to Elzie's gig in Beverley Hills we stopped off to collect his suit from the dry cleaners. The shop owner commented that he would charge rent next time. It turned out that the suit had been ready for collection for more than six months. 20 minutes later Elzie was performing his act in front of some of the wealthiest people in California. It struck me as bizarre; few would have known the performer entertaining them was homeless and few could have guessed that he would be sleeping on the city's pavements a few hours later.

Being white and spending periods in an area where whites don't go is always interesting. I'd seen South African townships many times and it can be frightening. In L.A., if you viewed events through your car window, it was like watching a scene from a movie or a hip-hop video. Up close it was more disturbing.

Generally the UK is a far more integrated society. There are far fewer obvious racial problems, though that is not to say that the situation is perfect. In the early 1980s a good friend in Birmingham was banned for life by a prominent cricket club in the city for refusing to play against a South African touring side during the Apartheid years. Richard Sargeant, a Bajan fast bowler turned academic who used to open the bowling with Joel Garner in his youth, thought long and hard about whether to play and, in the end, decided that his conscience would not allow it. Remarkably, and somewhat disappointingly, this particular club's committee took the decision to ban him.

Still, the situation does not bear much comparison with the U.S.. Funerals in ghettos, and the pattern in which they occur, are predictable. Martin Luther King Hospital became a name heard too frequently. Its mortuary was a place visited by too many parents as they came to identify their kids. It costs $4,600 to bury a body. The money is hardly ever available. Raising cash for funerals is a constant issue.

Typically this would mean members of the team calling on the help of the prettiest girls they knew, asking them to spend a day, or sometimes two, on the busiest roads in the area holding up banners offering to wash cars for cash. Not a sophisticated tactic perhaps. But effective nevertheless. Often the best area to raise money was one that carried the tag 'EJ', short for 'Execution Junction' due to its popularity with drive-by shootings. A damn dangerous place to be, but safety takes a back seat in those circumstances.

Planned overseas excursions for the Homies & the POPz have recently become difficult to organise due to costs incurred in taking the squad. Several financial offers to pick up the tab for such tours have failed to materialise into actual cash. A team tour to Australia was recently pulled at the last moment leaving many youngsters distraught. Hopefully in the future the opportunity to go down-under will resurface. Without cricket and support through organized activity many of these kids are unlikely ever to leave California. Players who have travelled to the UK in the past gained the invaluable experience of other cultures. Many times I've heard them say what a massive impact it had on their life. It showed them that their own lives need not take the path of many other Compton teenagers.

The team and the many players involved within it need constant encouragement if they are to grow as people. If anything is an advertisement for cricket, and an indicator of what a sport can do for people, especially youngsters, it's the Homies & the POPz.

An example of a Compton cricket session would include match situations where batsmen bat in pairs. It guaranteed they learned to communicate with each other. They learned to trust the judgment of others. Americans are no different to any other nation in that they would rather play than practice. It's even more important in this district. If nothing else it teaches those involved how to keep their eye on the ball, something they've failed to do in everyday life. Over time you saw improved behaviour, a more positive outlook and structure beginning to fill a normal week. Some see a real improvement in their quality of life.

All has not gone smoothly for the Homies and the POPz, however. They played fewer fixtures as the original stalwarts of the team have grown up. What had once been a large squad of players started to dwindle. After a while it dropped off to about 20, and even some of those attended irregularly. In many ways it mirrored the problems of club cricket in England; young men get married and have kids and are no longer free to give up afternoons for a game. In many ways the dwindling numbers proved that the Homies & the POPz worked. Sometimes it was their careers that kept them away; many took jobs in construction, engineering or did warehouse work. The team had become a victim of its own success. These guys just didn't need it any more. They had escaped ghettos and gangs. They'd made it.

And sometimes the reasons were not so positive. The Homies & the POPz have lost two affiliated players in the last 12 months - aged 15 and 17 - to shootings - another was hit by an 18-wheeler truck at 80 mph. Not long back a teenage opening bat died after crashing his motorbike at speed whilst being chased by a car full of kids from a nearby neighbourhood. He died in his brother's arms. However, it's when kids have been shot dead that it hits home hardest. Imagine your own club losing players to such events. The Homies & the Popz have. It doesn't help recruitment.

All these issues combined to reduce those coming to the sessions in Compton. Yet it was a winning concept; I've seen it make a difference and it's too good to allow it to slide. I decided to keep returning to Compton to dedicate myself to the scheme's success. Trials were organized so different squads could be formed; little pockets of players. Learning a sport, being kept busy in a positive environment, this scheme should be extended to include areas such as Morrovia, Pasadena and Duarte. We could spread the gospel further that way.

Kids with issues rarely turn up in groups. Sometimes they drift into the park, or meet someone else who is involved, and we can pick them up that way. Youngsters all hear about others finding jobs and stability and want to follow suit. It's not easy, but being affiliated with the Homies & the POPz helps people turn around their lives. It makes them wiser and calmer.

As I write this, it looks as if the numbers who regularly practice will stabilise at around an estimated 45. We are able to provide regular mentoring and we are playing a part in eradicating some of the problems on American streets. Mexican and black kids have started to appear. They play with white youngsters. Rarely would you see this kind of integration elsewhere in America. It reminds me of my time playing cricket in South Africa. Truly, cricket without boundaries. To me this shows more than anything that these schemes work.

It is not just a case of occupying people who would otherwise be up to no good. This is life changing. People who would in a previous time have fired bullets at one another are instead bonding together using a sport. They build a bond and a mutual understanding and respect which will be there for life.

The fundamental spirit of cricket - that spirit that is only partially able to be written into the Laws of the game - is so positive for these young people. They learn that they have to respect authority and the decisions of other people. They learn about team work; that they have to work together, turn up on time and play their part if everyone is to succeed. They learn to walk away from trouble. And they learn about the spirit of fair play.

Would that be the case if I were to coach football? I don't think so. Increasingly we've watched as soccer has become a game in which players are expected to cheat. When was the last time you saw a player admit that the throw-in should be awarded to the other side? Or admit they were off-side? Or accept a penalty without reacting as if the referee had just stolen their car, their wife and their first born child? Mind you, I once sat in a PCA meeting where Mike Garnham, the tenacious Leicester wicket-keeper stood up and said that if he edged a ball when batting and 'walked' before the umpire had made their decision, he would be given a bollocking when he returned to the changing room.

Having been on both sides of the fence as a top sportsman who 'had it all' to rock bottom, living under the night sky in inner-city Los Angeles, I can only tell you my experiences - and those tell me that fulfilment is spiritual and is vital to turning lives around.

Funding trips to the U.S. became a real issue. I had poured pretty much my last money into it. Every penny. I had been living on collateral for some time whilst I developed this concept; both financially and spiritually. Ironic really; by trying to help those with nothing I became one of them. There are rich individuals who provide generously, but in the end it will need government involvement on a large scale to solve these issues. Despite what people say, many of the rich do care. No-one wants to see society run by gangs.

The ICC provided me with a leaflet for the kids. It's the best I've seen yet; the clearest in explaining the rules of cricket to kids who've never seen the game played and may well initially struggle to grasp the rules. You have to take into account that for many kids English isn't their first language. This is a city in which 120 different languages are spoken, and which covers 57 districts. This additional resource will help Ted mentor young people who'll spread the gospel of cricket weekly in eight Los Angeles Schools.

The cricket and educational activity will hopefully act as the catalyst towards cricket becoming a regular part of the Los Angeles curriculum across all schools. Expansion plans are in place should we receive the green light after the pilot scheme. In addition to cricket taking place during school hours there have been a number cricket days held at weekends with over 100 kids attending. I believe over time the LAPD will notice a noticeable reduction in trouble on the street.

Ted has proved to be a tireless worker for the dispossessed. He is highly intelligent and has brilliant skills of communication. He's marched and demonstrated for other peoples' rights more times than I can remember. He even took a shot in the chest once. The rubber bullets, fired by police during a silent demonstration march in L.A., saw him fall to the ground draped in the stars and stripes flag he carried; an ironic and symbolic moment. A picture of the incident made the front page of the *L.A Times*.

Given time, Americans will wake up and understand what cricket can teach them. Congratulations must go to those who stuck with the ideas and the team, especially Katy Haber. Cricket changed vulnerable kids' lives for ever. It took them out of dangerous environments and allowed them to travel and express themselves in a way they never imagined possible. They didn't know cricket existed until Katy introduced Ted to it at Beverly Hills cricket club.

The Homies & the POPz team has become famous across the United States and was praised by then President Bill Clinton and his Vice-President Al Gore for offering young people a viable alternative to a life of drugs and violence. It would be good if everyone involved were allowed to take things yet further. Any help with funding, be it from the ICC or from private sources, would make an enormous difference.

Has it been worth it? Of course it has. Categorically, yes. How do you put a price on intervening in a life headed in the wrong direction and turning it around? Not everything that counts can be counted. Recent times in L.A. have seen me awarded the Certificate of Appreciation for work carried out in these ghetto areas. I'm still the only non-American citizen to receive such an accolade. It means more to me than any championship winners medals.

Compton Revisited

Standing in this park in Compton I smell the familiar aroma of marijuana creeping across the field from the basketball area. It's 1pm and the Homies & the POPz cricket squad have started to arrive; a lively bunch of seasoned Latino, Hispanic, black and Mexican Californians talk the talk, catching up on news.

To the left there's a huge sandpit. It used to be a pond, but after the local authorities drained it in the search for bodies, it has never been refilled. They found rather more than they were bargaining for; 42 body parts in all, I'm told. Along with various knives, chains and guns.

I'm glad there are only roads to two sides of the park; it reduces the chances of drive-by shootings. That makes me think of all the dangerous situations I have found myself in during my life; avoiding fast cricket balls has been the least of my worries.

Supermarket trolleys are pushed under trees nearby. They contain three car batteries which feed the sound system; the accompaniment to our afternoon. Music blasts out; 2Pac. The irony hits me again. The man is still portrayed by the media as the typical gang member, but he had actually renounced violence and gang culture by the time of his bloody death. I hope all these kids remember that.

It's interesting to note that both 2Pac and Tookie Williams had their ashes scattered in Soweto; a place I know well from my days coaching in South Africa as an 18 year-old; an experience that helped shape what I do now. The similarities and links between Soweto and L.A. are stronger than you may think.

It is a million miles from where I thought life might take me. But it's where I belong.

The story of the Homies & the POPz is ongoing. Funding is required if we are to wean more people away from the gangs and into structured and positive activities. I've seen it work; I know it can make a difference.

It's crossed my mind more than once that my relationship with these young people is symbiotic. Perhaps they help me as much as I help them. I know that there was a self-destructive element within me that caused plenty of trouble, but I also know that it's brought me a lot of great memories. I know how hard it was to conquer demons. It didn't start to happen until I eradicated certain people from my daily life. I hope it's also given me the insight into understanding what other people are going through. That's the key for all my work now. Turning the bad into good.

It pleases me that Cricket Without Boundaries continues to do good work. I'm proud of the difference it has made both in Los Angeles with the Homies & the Popz and in the United Kingdom, thanks to the Prince's Trust. It remains the template for everything I want to achieve.

*   *   *

I said at the start of this book that I can't promise a happy ending. Life isn't like that. A happy ending is just a story with a chapter missing. Real life just isn't so neat.

Perhaps, if I had set out to write a sports book, the last chapter would end with me on the balcony at Lord's, drinking champagne from the Cup with team-mates and celebrating my Man Of The Match performance . As I said though, this isn't that sort of book. And it hasn't been that sort of life.

My own life - like yours, I suspect - is also still a work in progress. I've recently learned that I am to become a father for the fourth time. Wonderful news.

I'm very aware that life gave me a second chance. I intend to seize it. But I don't intend to forget everything that I've learned. But that's not an ending. Only a new beginning. And another story...

THE PINNACLE BEFORE THE FALL

My Man of the Match performance to win a Lord's final should be the greatest moment of my life, surpassing all others. And of course, it was wonderful - but the satisfaction I gain from my work with young people, helping to change the course of their lives away from the destructive course my own took for a number of years, will always be more important to me.

Acknowledgments

Thanks to...

Corrina for taking the main jacket picture, also to Simon Donald - 'The Mighty Viz' - for taking the time to write the Foreword. Thank you to another close school friend, Angela Jenkison, who re-introduced Simon and me after a 20-year gap. Thanks to George Dobell for his professionalism, humour and his linking and culling skills which made this writing easier to compile. To "B" for friendship, security and laughter. Gratitude to the "Bajan Sergeant" at Café Nero in Harborne, England for his constant encouragement, humour and wit, also to the Nero staff. Also to the staff at the Side Walk Café on Venice Beach Boardwalk.

Sincere thanks to friends spread far and wide for whom a lot of words in this book will strike a note. To all at Know The Score Books, especially Simon Lowe. THANX 2 Mikey 4 photo selection advice. Gratitude to mom, dad and my brothers for being a constant reassuring presence throughout life. Thanks to my kids, Oliver, Mikey and Levi, for many priceless moments which remain ingrained in the memory - a second thank you to all three of you for seeing humour at times when I no longer could. And for understanding, laughing and never criticizing. Ayeisha and Satish - remember to eat your vegetables, to do all your homework and remember your father loves you.

Thanks to the genuine people who encouraged and helped me in any amount of ways at a time when I was learning that life is not a lucky dip where a prize is guaranteed. Also thanks to *The Birmingham Post & Mail*, Paul Davies, Kate Kelly, Graham and Diana Morris, Roger Wootton, Robert Brooke and Abi Dollery. And thanks to all my teammates over the years; there'll always be masses more that unites us than divides - mine's a black Sambucca! Genuine thanks to the Professional Cricketers' Association for doing everything they did to stabilise things. Bob Woolmer RIP, for touching us with such spirit and knowledge when he came into our lives.

Thanks to friends and supporters around the world who "smile like they mean it." I've seen the spirit of cricket achieve amazing things in unexpected places. America has thrown up many such examples through my work with Ted Hayes, a man who's taught me so much. I thank Ted for the countless times he's informed me as to whether or not we're safe in L.A - and his uncanny knack of getting us out of trouble. I look forward to continuing our joint aspirations.

And a big thank you goes to Janette for seeing sense at a stage when I'd worked out that sense isn't common. I look forward to our all our future experiences, including Kizzi.

Some time back I spoke to a well known BBC sports journalist. He told me that writing this book should be "cathartic." I didn't know what he meant at the time. But it was...

P.A.S
March 2007